MW01100482

About the author: Bruce O'Hara is the director and founder of Work Well, Canada's first Work Option Resource Centre. Over the past three years he has helped hundreds of Canadians negotiate more flexible working arrangements—including many people who said, "My employer will **never** give me what I want." *Put Work In Its Place* is his second book.

Bruce O'Hara works three days a week—and loves it!

PUT WORK IN ITS PLACE

How to Redesign Your Job
to Fit Your Life

**The Complete Guide
to the Flexible Work Place**
by Bruce O'Hara

Work Well Publications
Victoria, B.C.

Copyright © 1988 Bruce O'Hara

All rights reserved—no part of this book may be reproduced in any form without permission in writing from the publisher, except by a reviewer who wishes to quote brief passages in connection with a review written for inclusion in a magazine or newspaper.

Canadian Cataloguing in Publication Data

O'Hara, Bruce, 1952-
    Put work in its place

    Bibliography: p. 251
    ISBN 0-9693286-0-5

    1. Hours of labour, Flexible. 2. Job sharing. 3. Part-time employment. 4. Telecommuting. I. Title.

HD5109.O53 1988   331.25'72   C88-091058-5

Edited by Judith Alldritt McDowell
Cartoons by Graham Harrop
Cover design by Dee van Straaten
Printed by Hignell Printing, Winnipeg.

Acknowledgments

The author wishes to thank the design team that produced this volume.

- Judith Alldritt McDowell edited the book from start to finish and comforted and encouraged me at times when it seemed that the text would never be clear or concise — or finished.

- Kathy English wrote the "Spotlights" in Step Two.

- Graham Harrop created the delightful cartoons.

- Dee van Straaten designed the cover.

- Kathie Gibson co-ordinated layout design and production.

- Karen Goodwin at Desktop Publishing Ltd. did all the typesetting electronically.

The contributions of the following individuals and groups also deserve acknowledgment:

- all the individuals and organizations who have shared with us their experience of the benefits and difficulties of flexible work scheduling; in particular, we are grateful to those individuals whose stories appear as "Spotlights."

- all the clients of the Work Well Work Option Resource Centre in Victoria, B.C.; their creativity and persistence in creating new balance in their lives has inspired us.

- Work Well staff members Sylvia Fields, Frances Hunter, Pauline Shepherd, Roseanna Waldock and Barry Walters for pitching in so enthusiastically whenever they were called upon to assist.

- Victoria Work Well Society board members Doug Crow, Jane Dewing, David McLean, Rosemarie Schmidt, Johan Schuyff, David Stott, Diane Woodman and Pat Young for their encouragement, advice and service.

Put Work In Its Place was made possible by funding from the Innovations Program of the Government of Canada, Department of Employment and Immigration.

Table of Contents

How to Use This Book

In 1955, roughly 70 per cent of households in Canada consisted of a husband who worked full-time outside the home, a wife who was a full-time homemaker and one or more children. The standard 40-hour work week was a response to this homogeneous family pattern. It was designed to meet the needs of men with housewives. The standard one-size-fits-all work schedule became part of the structure of the work place first as a habit, then as an assumption and finally as an institution—even as the family pattern it was meant to serve was disappearing.

Today, only seven per cent of Canadian households fit the once typical pattern of a working husband supporting a homemaker and children. Over 40 per cent of the work force are now female. Over 50 per cent of the mothers of young children work outside the home. Forty per cent of full-time workers have a spouse who also works full-time. A 1985 survey by the Conference Board of Canada found that 31 per cent of Canadian workers would prefer to work less, even if it meant earning less, and that a majority of working Canadians would like to change their working hours in some way.

Many Canadians feel "burned out" from working more than they want to. Many are discovering that they want more time for family, for volunteer work, for travel, for hobbies—for living. If you are one of those individuals—or think you might be—this book is for you.

During the last 15 years, a whole range of practical new working arrangements, collectively called work time options or simply work options, have gradually come into use. Work options are voluntary, employee-initiated arrangements to reduce or restructure work times. In contrast to traditional part-time work, work options usually carry with them hourly rates of pay equal to full-time, a fair share of fringe benefits and full employment rights. The range of options now in use includes job sharing, permanent part-time, leaves of absence, V-Time, banked overtime, phased retirement, flexitime, the compressed work week, and telecommuting.

If designed and used appropriately, any of these options can benefit both employees and employers. Within the nine standard options, there are several possible variations. Almost any imaginable schedule can be accommodated.

Because work options are innovative and not well known, they are not widely available in Canada — at least not yet. However, work options are spreading fast because of their practicality and their proven ability to satisfy the needs of both employees and employers. In the vast majority of cases, this change is being initiated by individual employees rather than by government, unions or top management. In other words, work options are winning credibility in the work place precisely because people like you are asking for what they want in a work schedule — and getting it.

Work Well is Canada's first Work Option Resource Centre. Over the past three years, Work Well has helped many Canadians arrange new working hours that better meet their needs. So far, three general rules of thumb have emerged from that experience:

1. You are more likely to get what you want in a work schedule if you take the time to find out exactly what you want and need.

2. If you begin by investigating the full range of options available, you will be in a better position to select the option that best suits your needs.

3. A comprehensive written proposal will greatly increase your chances of getting what you want.

Put Work In Its Place has been designed to take the reader through the seven-step process that clients at the Work Well centre have found to be most effective.

Step One: Thinking Clearly About Work examines the cultural baggage we all carry with us about work. It is designed to help you free yourself from outdated attitudes to work so that you can choose the schedule you really want.

Step Two: Surveying Your Options describes nine new types of work schedule. The introduction to Step Two can help you quickly identify which option(s) will best suit your needs. Alternatively, you can window-shop through all nine. Each chapter in Step Two deals with one of the nine standard work options. The chapters include criteria for deciding if that option is appropriate for you and your job and a "spotlight" or mini-profile of the option in practice. If you read all the spotlights, you will have a good picture of the basic options and how they can be combined or modified to meet a great diversity of personal needs.

Step Three: Choosing Your Time is designed to help you create a new balance in your life that better reflects your personal priorities.

Step Four: Deciding About Money helps you deal creatively with the financial implications of changing your work schedule.

Step Five: Designing A Program takes you through the process of redesigning your job so that you can get the work schedule you want and still meet your employer's needs. Each chapter in Step Five contains specific advice on one of the nine work options.

Step Six: Getting What You Want explains how to produce a successful proposal for a new work schedule.

Step Seven: Putting Work In Its Place shows how to get your proposal approved quickly and how to implement your new schedule in a way that will encourage greater flexibility in your work place.

Special Cases/Further Resources expands on a number of special issues related to flexible work options.

A healthy balance between work and personal life is so satisfying and so rewarding that those who have achieved it often find it hard to believe they were ever willing to settle for less. They are also aware that the benefits of putting work in its place are not merely self-centred; the whole and happy person is an asset to families, friends, co-workers and the community.

Futurists estimate that the flexible working arrangements described in this book will be the norm for almost everyone within 20 to 25 years. You don't have to wait that long; you have in front of you a complete tool kit for achieving freedom, flexibility and balance — now.

Getting the balance you want in life is not an easy process or a quick one. It requires effort and careful thought. In many cases, success also requires courage and persistence. Time and time again, however, those who have been through the process report that the results are well worth the effort.

Bruce O'Hara

Step One

Thinking Clearly About Work

Sorting Out the Baggage of the Past

Work is a lot like sex—it's hard to think clearly about it when your emotions are involved. Although work is primarily a source of income, it also has a big influence on our feelings. It affects our sense of self-worth and our sense of who we are. We structure our time around our work, and work also determines many of our social contacts.

It's hard to think clearly about work because the subject is surrounded with emotionally charged and frequently contradictory ideas, images, values and judgments. Before we can know what we really think about work, we have to sort through all the things we've been told we "should" think and feel.

Many of our ideas about work reflect deep-seated values from the past, some of which have outlived their usefulness. The values we attach to work are more than a response to present-day realities; in large part, they are a response to "voices" from the various stages of human history.

Work in the Hunter/Gatherer Economy

For upwards of one million years, or more than 99 per cent of our history on this planet, human beings lived in small nomadic tribes that hunted and foraged for food. They had few possessions because every possession was an extra burden to carry as they moved around from place to place in search of food.

As a way of gathering food, the nomadic life was inefficient because the land could support only a few people per acre. However, it was very efficient in terms of work, because people ate only what nature freely provided. Anthropologist Marshall Sahlins has estimated that nomadic people spent an average of 20 to 25 hours per week on activities we would call "work."

For the vast majority of human history, then, people worked only half the time we work today. If there were a work load determined by our genetic make up or natural selection, it would be only 20 to 25 hours per week. If you are one of those people who feel like you've worked enough by Wednesday afternoon, you may be hearing an ancient voice from deep within your psyche. You may be responding to a genetic prompting based on a million years of history.

Work in the Agricultural Economy

Roughly ten thousand years ago, human beings ceased living as nomads; they started planting crops and tending animals. Because people moved around much less, it made sense to accumulate more possessions. Although growing food required more work, the supply was more dependable. It also meant that more people could survive on a smaller area of land.

The agricultural era ended about two hundred years ago with the coming of the industrial revolution, but many of our values about religion, family and work originate from this time. In an agricultural economy, work was not the only, or even the most important, element in people's lives. Other spheres of activity were of equal or greater value.

Religion, for example, was extremely important. In those days, religion involved a collective, communal web of activities that required active participation. During the Middle Ages there were 200 religious holidays per year, and most of the population of Europe did no work on those days.

The extended family structure meant that nurturing the young, tending the old and caring for the sick all took place within the family. Celebration and self-expression were also public, participatory activities. Work was only one of a range of activities through which individuals developed a sense of identity, worth and purpose.

The strong emotional values we attach to family and church may seem out of proportion to the time we actually spend on these activities today. However, it is not so disproportionate if we see these values as a hungering for communal structures that we once had and have lost.

Prior to the industrial revolution, people satisfied most of their economic needs through a complex social contract rather than through monetary exchanges. The vast majority of people were either self-employed or worked within a larger economic unit in which no cash traded hands.

Working for wages was considered to be one step away from slavery. People thought of wage labour in much the same way we think of prostitution — as an intrusion of economic values into an area that is more properly personal. The lingering notion that paid work creates "wage slaves" and the idea that paid activities are not as "pure" as activities we do for free both reflect the values of pre-industrial society.

Work in the Industrial Economy

Around the year 1800, the introduction of steam power and the spread of the factory system transformed the economic base of society and heralded the death of rural culture. By 1850, the average work week had shot up to 60 hours. This unprecedented obsession with work trivialized and pushed aside activities which previously had enjoyed equal social value.

In the first half of this century, the harshness of the industrial economy began to soften. The average work week fell from roughly 60 hours to around 40. Wages rose to the point where a single wage earner could support himself, a spouse and children. A well-defined division of sex roles occurred; the man worked outside the home, and the woman worked inside the home.

In the new value system which arose with industrialization, paid work became the most important activity in the culture. It supplanted activities that were formerly part of a social matrix. Child care became the province of professional teachers, and caring for the infirm, the domain of the medical profession. Self-expression devolved into a paid entertainment industry. Human concern and support became the bailiwick of counsellors and therapists. Sport was largely given over to professional athletes. Even charity became a professional activity. Unpaid activities had little status; people became "just" housewives or "just" volunteers.

We have grown up in an industrial society whose attitudes to work are abnormal because they are one-sided. The industrial era has brought tremendous technical and economic progress (none of us would like to return to the Middle Ages), but this progress has been purchased at the price of emotional wholeness.

Industrial man (or woman) is in many ways an emotional cripple. Whereas self-worth and a sense of belonging once stood on several legs, they now frequently totter uncertainly on the one leg of our relationship to work. As Erich Fromm points out in *The Sane Society*, it is difficult to be sane in an insane society. It is unfair to consider workaholics as somehow "deviant" in our culture. In a culture that is obsessed with work, workaholics are individuals who in fact follow the rules of the culture too well. They are people who have failed to rebel against becoming in Marcuse's phrase "one dimensional man."

Work in the Service Economy

In the twentieth century, rising labour costs have led increasingly to the use of machines that are designed to replace human labour in the production process. Because fewer and fewer workers are needed to make things, more and more of the work force became involved in selling things and providing services—education, banking, entertainment, health care, and so on.

As the economy shifts away from production and towards services, most of the new jobs are being created in areas that have traditionally employed women. Starting in about 1950, women began entering the labour force in large numbers. By 1987, women were filling three out of four new jobs.

To some extent, we are still in the transition from an industrial economy to a service economy, and thus we find ourselves caught between two worlds. Our systems of work scheduling are largely designed for an industrial era in which the work force was made up of men with housewives.

In the 1950s, the male wage earner in the family worked 40 or 50 hours per week outside the home while his spouse spent a similar amount of time on housework and child care. The rest of the time was available for family activities and entertainment. This was the dominant social pattern.

A different social pattern has been emerging in the 1980s as a result of rising expectations and inflation in the cost of living. Today, husbands and wives both work 40 or 50 hours per week outside the home, and their "free time" goes to housework. Although the new pattern has raised family income, it has also brought increasing levels of divorce, alcoholism, child abuse, suicide, stress-related illness and psychiatric disorders.

As we move from an industry-based economy to a service-based economy, the mismatch between the structures of the work place and the needs of the work force can be expected to cause increasing levels of social stress. In the 1980s, many of us feel like square pegs in round holes. And we are.

Work in the Economy of the Future

The work place continues to change with increasing rapidity. Current estimates indicate that automation and computers will eliminate roughly one-quarter of current jobs before the year 2020. Women are expected to continue entering the work force in large numbers.

... CERTAINLY IT'S A DEPARTURE FROM THE MOTHER-
WORKS-FATHER-STAYS-HOME   FATHER-WORKS-
MOTHER-STAYS-HOME SYNDROME...

These trends are accompanied by some startling demographic changes. As a result of the 1950s "baby boom," large numbers of young people entered the labour force each year from the late sixties until the mid-eighties. However, the "baby bust" that followed the introduction of "the pill" in the early sixties means that very few young people will be entering the labour market in the near future. In fact, some furturists estimate that over the next twenty years, more people will be leaving the labour force than entering it. John Naisbitt, author of *Re-inventing the Corporation*, estimates that the baby bust effect will result in a sharp decrease in unemployment over the next decade, despite the effects of automation.

Naisbitt also points out that in a fast-changing service economy, a corporation's most important asset is no longer its machinery or its financial base, but its employees. Companies that attract and retain the best people will be at an advantage. If unemployment declines, companies will be under increasing pressure to provide flexible work arrangements and ongoing staff development in order to compete for the best people.

Our ideas are changing along with the economy. In his book *New Rules,* pollster Daniel Yankelovich documents a profound shift in social values. North Americans used to operate primarily out of what he terms an "ethic of success?" For most people, being successful—having a big car, a "good" job, a fancy house and the envy of one's neighbours—was the goal of life.

Increasingly, however, North Americans are shifting to what Yankelovich calls an "ethic of self-fulfillment." Instead of asking "How can I be successful?" people are asking "What gives meaning, satisfaction and value to my life?" Instead of assuming that some pre-packaged picture of "success" will make them happy, people are starting to make their own decisions about what is most important in life. Today, many of these individuals are asking for new work schedules, and more can be expected to do so in the years to come.

Several futurists have estimated that by the early 2000s the average work week will fall to 20 hours per week. A new social pattern is expected to develop in which husbands and wives will both work about 20 to 25 hours per week for pay, spend a like amount of time on domestic tasks and have the rest of the time available for family activities and entertainment.

The good news is that more sensible work schedules are on their way. The bad news is that it may take 15 years before they are widely available. If you are not prepared to wait that long, this book is for you.

Summary

What lessons can we derive from history that can guide us in developing a healthy attitude toward work?

It's okay to want to work less. For the greater part of human history, people have worked less than they do now. For all we know, an aptitude for more leisure may be built into our genes.

It's okay to want to work. People often feel guilty for working when work is not financially necessary. However, in a society that is as obsessed with work as our society is, it is important to recognize that work is one of the few legitimate paths to status, social connection and a sense of self-worth.

It's okay to want not to work. History tells us that paid work doesn't have to be the centre of life. There are many ways to make a contribution to the community. We needn't allow our own cultural bias to blind us to other possibilities for self-fulfillment.

Change isn't easy. We live in a culture that assumes there is something wrong with people who are not devoted to work. Your boss may share this view. In these circumstances, change requires persistence, patience and a willingness to fight against the dead hand of the past.

The sexual revolution is only half over. Women have moved into the work force in large numbers, but they are working within structures designed for men. Intellectually, men have accepted the idea that they should be more involved with parenting and housework. In practice, however, men are still locked into attitudes and work place structures that make work the focus of their lives. Until men are also liberated, women's liberation will have little practical value.

Balance is important to your health. People are more likely to remain sane and happy when they have a number of meaningful roles and activities. Our society tends to be emotionally unhealthy because many people establish their identities almost exclusively through work.

You are not alone. A recent Conference Board of Canada survey found that about one-third of working Canadians would like to work less. If you would like to change the role of work in your life, your ideas are not aberrant; they are the way of the future.

Step Two

Surveying Your Options

Nine Ways to Have the Best of Both Worlds

In extended trials in U.S., European and Canadian companies, the following nine work options have proved their usefulness as practical alternatives to the 40-hour work week.

Job Sharing: two or more persons share one full-time position, with salary and benefits prorated.

Permanent Part-Time: less than full-time, but with seniority rights, promotion opportunities, prorated benefits and hourly rates of pay equal to full-time.

Leaves of Absence: authorized periods of time away from work without loss of employment rights.

V-Time: a voluntary, time/income trade off that allows employees to reduce work hours by 5, 10, 20 or 50 per cent for a specified period of time.

Banked Overtime: programs whereby overtime pay may be converted to time off work.

Phased Retirement: employees approaching retirement qualify for a gradually reduced work week without loss or reduction of pension benefits.

Flexitime: employees work a standard number of hours per week with flexible starting and quitting times.

Compressed Work Week: employees work a standard number of hours within fewer days — for example, 40 hours per week in four 10-hour days.

Home Work/Telecommuting: employees work at home part of the time, in some cases communicating with the office through a computer linked to a telephone modem.

These are the standard work options available today. However, it is possible to develop minor or major variations of each option, depending upon the nature of the job, the needs of the employee and the needs of the employer. There is always room to "do it your way."

Narrowing the Field

Some work options will work better for you than others. Use these rules of thumb to help narrow the field.

- If you want to cut your work time by 40 per cent or more, look at **job sharing** and **permanent part-time.**

- If you want a slightly shorter work day or work week, consider **V-Time** or **permanent part-time.**

- If you want longer vacations or an extended period of time away from work, look at **V-Time** and **leaves of absence.**

- If you want to work fewer hours in the years before you retire, look at **phased retirement. Job sharing, permanent part-time, V-Time** or a **leave of absence** may also meet your needs.

- If you want to take time off in place of overtime pay, consider **banked overtime.**

- If you want to change your schedule without reducing your hours of work, look at **flexitime.** If you would prefer to work longer days but fewer of them, the **compressed work week** may suit your needs.

- If you want to do all or part of your work from home, then see **home work/telecommuting.**

When you've decided which option you like best, read the description of that option in Step Two. If you aren't sure how much time you need or how large a cut in hours you can afford, complete Steps Three and Four first. Then go to Step Two.

The information in Step Two will help you decide if the option is right for you and how well it would work in your job. If two or more options seem equally workable, look at them again with the following questions in mind.

- *How well does the option suit your needs?*

- *How easy would it be to sell your employer on it?*

Job Sharing

Job sharing is a work arrangement in which two or more (but usually two) people agree to share the duties, wages and benefits of one full-time job. Although job sharers work part-time, the job remains a full-time position in the eyes of the employer.

Job sharing first became popular in Europe after the Second World War. An estimated three to four per cent of European workers share their jobs: In Britain 25,000 job sharers work at Barclays Bank alone. About a dozen years ago, the job sharing concept caught on in the U.S.: between one and two per cent of Americans now share their jobs. However, only in the last few years has job sharing started to catch on in Canada.

So far in this country, job sharing is most popular with professionals, especially teachers and nurses, and with women. However, evidence from Europe and the U.S. suggests that job sharing is appropriate for a wide range of occupations. As the idea becomes more accepted and job sharing becomes more generally available, more men also start to use the option.

People decide to job share for wide variety of reasons, but the most common one is a desire to have more time for child care at home. Parents of young children often find full-time work incompatible with the demands of home and family.

Many women leave the work force while their children are young, and they often have a hard time re-entering the work force at a later date. Job sharing avoids this problem by allowing mothers of young children to keep their position at work while having more time to spend at home. Today, fathers also want more time to spend with their children.

Job sharing also appeals to people who need large blocks of time to devote to some activity outside the work place. This includes artists and writers and people who are starting their own business. People who want to upgrade their skills or develop a new career may need time during the day to attend courses at college or university.

People in high stress jobs may decide to job share for health reasons. Job sharing may also be the answer for people whose work is highly repetitive and boring or for an older person seeking a comfortable re-entry into the work force. If appropriate pension arrangements are available, job sharing can be an ideal way to phase into retirement gradually.

There are many different ways to share a job. In some arrangements, the partners divide the duties of the job along well-defined lines and work almost independently of one another. In other arrangements, the partners share all duties and work closely together as a team. Sometimes, but not always, one partner routinely fills in if the other partner is ill. Many job sharers trade blocks of time with each other in order to get longer vacations or in order to attend special events; in other arrangements, such trading is discouraged or expressly forbidden. Schedules vary greatly as well. Some job sharers work half-days; others work half-weeks or alternate weeks. Some work alternate months or even alternate years. Sometimes job sharers divide hours unequally; for example, one partner might work three days per week, and the other partner would work the remaining two days. Occasionally, three people will share two full-time jobs. In Victoria, B.C., three teachers successfully shared two full-time teaching positions: two worked 60 per cent of the time, and the other worked 80 per cent.

Parent/student job sharing is another interesting variation on the job sharing model. In parent/student job sharing, a parent of school-age children shares a job with a university or college student. The parent works full-time except during Christmas, Easter and summer holidays, at which times the student takes over. The parent gets time with the children when they are away from school, and the student earns money for educational expenses. In "Job Sharing for Youth" programs, organizations make job sharing available as an option to all entry-level employees, as long as the job sharing partner is an unemployed young person. Job Sharing for Youth programs give young people a chance to enter the work force gradually; they are also an ideal form of job training because the young person gets instruction and back-up from the experienced partner.

Job sharing and work sharing are not the same, although the two terms are often used interchangeably. Job sharing is a voluntary arrangement which individual employees may request in order to meet their personal needs for additional free time. Work sharing is an involuntary arrangement in which the employer attempts to avoid layoffs by cutting hours of work, usually with the agreement of the union. Work sharing doesn't necessarily mean that two workers share the duties of a specific job. In fact, most work sharing programs involve an across-the-board cut in the hours of all employees.

When discussing job sharing with your co-workers, your union or your supervisor, it is often important to make sure that they understand the crucial differences between job sharing and work sharing.

What Do Employers Think of Job Sharing?

Today, more and more employers are sympathetic to the idea of job sharing. Those who are naturally innovative or who have had some experience of job sharing are usually easy to persuade. Employers who have already tried job sharing are aware of the advantages that come from having the benefit of two people's ideas, energy and enthusiasm.

Nevertheless, most potential job sharers are pioneers who must work hard to convince employers that the arrangement will be of mutual benefit. Some employers are naturally conservative and suspicious of change. They will be reluctant to accept job sharing because they have never tried it and don't understand it. In most cases, their reluctance is based on legitimate concerns. Will job sharing disrupt the smooth operation of the work involved? Will the work get done as needed without delay or confusion? Will other workers' schedules and ability to carry out their jobs be affected? Will job sharing mean more work for management personnel? Will job sharing cost the company more money for employee benefits and training programs?

If you hope to convince your employer to let you share your job, even on a trial basis, you would be wise to design a program which clearly addresses these concerns and to present your request in the form of a written proposal.

What Do Unions Think of Job Sharing?

Many unions, particularly those with a high proportion of female members, are becoming sensitive to the need for alternate work arrangements. Some unions will actively campaign for the right to job share, but others still oppose job sharing because they equate it with part-time work. Unions object to part-time work because it traditionally involved penalties for the employee in terms of rights, benefits and job security.

Union contracts that rule out part-time work make job sharing difficult or impossible. However, as job sharing becomes more popular and accepted, unions are beginning to recognize the need to support members who request job sharing arrangements. This support can and should take the form of negotiating contract terms that create job sharing opportunities with full employment rights, equal hourly rates of pay and prorated benefit packages.

Would Job Sharing Suit Your Needs?

The process of setting up a job sharing arrangement may involve a considerable amount of time, persuasion and paperwork. It also involves a significant loss of income. Before you begin, it is important to consider your motives and your ability to deal with all the circumstances involved in sharing a job.

If you are thinking of sharing your job, you should look closely at your personal needs in the areas of time, money, career development, authority and responsibility, and work habits.

TIME

Job sharing generally works best when both partners keep to a regular work schedule. Your schedule may involve working half-days, half-weeks or even half-years, but it should be consistent and predictable in order to avoid confusing co-workers, clients or supervisors.

The option of trading time with a partner makes job sharing more flexible than most traditional forms of part-time work, but if you prefer a highly fluid schedule, you may feel dissatisfied in a job sharing arrangement. If you are looking for a great deal of freedom to determine when and how much you work, you would be better off working "on call" or as a self-employed contractor or consultant.

For help in assessing your needs for time, see Step Three.

MONEY

Because most job sharing arrangements involve working half-time and earning half-pay, you'll find it easier if you have a relatively well-paid job or a working spouse who is earning a good salary. If not, you'll have to look carefully at ways to limit your expenses enough to get by on a reduced income. For more information about money needs, see Step Four.

CAREER DEVELOPMENT

For people who don't want to give up work in order to have a family or pursue outside interests, job sharing can be an ideal compromise, but there is a cost involved. Few job sharers get promoted unless they are willing to return to work full-time. This is not to say that job sharers never get promoted; sometimes two heads are so much better than one that job sharers create an unbeatable combina-

Spotlight on Job Sharing

Maureen Dewhurst and Jill Evans job share the position of Program Placement Officer at Western Community Outreach, an employment centre near Victoria. As counsellors, they match the skills and interests of special needs clients with wage-subsidized employment opportunities. Once a contract has been negotiated, Maureen and Jill continue to monitor the placement and provide ongoing support to their clients.

Maureen and Jill split the week between them. One partner works Monday and Tuesday, and the other works Thursday and Friday. They work together on Wednesday morning and spend part of this "cross-over" time up-dating each other on new contracts and other client-related information. Their schedules are designed so that they each get an equal number of statutory holidays, and they also get complete benefit packages, prorated for half-time.

Maureen used to administer the program by herself on a full-time basis. However, at one point she came close to resigning because of the stress associated with the job and her desire to spend more time with her young son. Her supervisor suggested that she follow the example of another staff member and try job sharing.

Maureen's supervisor knew that compatibility is a key factor in successful job sharing, so she advised Maureen to participate in the selection of her job sharing partner. Maureen reviewed resumes and conducted her own interview with short-listed candidates.

After more than a year of job sharing, Maureen and Jill agree that their partnership works because "they are on the same wave length." They also share a good sense of humor, and they trust each other to do the job well. Since they began job sharing, other staff have commented on their energy and productivity. According to one staff member, the position they share is so demanding that job sharing is the only way anyone could handle it.

The arrangement has only one minor drawback. Since Maureen and Jill work different days of the week each month, other staff members sometimes find it hard to remember which partner will be in the office on a particular day without first consulting the appointment book.

Today, Maureen is glad she chose job sharing instead of resigning. "I've never been happier in any job!" she says. "It's the best office I have ever worked in."

tion. However, experience to date indicates that employers are more likely to promote individual full-time workers than job sharing teams.

It's important to question yourself carefully on this point. If getting ahead in your job or your profession is important to you, you may find that job sharing is not in your best interest.

AUTHORITY AND RESPONSIBILITY

Some people find satisfaction in having the authority that goes with full responsibility for important tasks or projects. These people are "independents" who often have difficulty working in cooperative situations where they are required to share responsibility and authority. They enjoy the status, attention and rewards that go with being "the boss." Their motivation depends to a large extent on getting full credit for individual achievements. They like clearly demarcated areas of responsibility and will object to taking the blame for someone else's errors.

Other people prefer working shoulder to shoulder in a team setting where there is a constant exchange of ideas and no one person is "in charge." These people can handle the process of sharing responsibility for decisions and the lack of individual authority that is a feature of a cooperative working arrangement. They are more concerned about getting good results than about who gets either the credit or the blame. They seem relatively indifferent to the kudos that goes with a "star" performance. They are also willing to shoulder part of the blame for problems, even though they might not be directly responsible.

Before setting up a job sharing arrangement, it's important to establish which of these two types you most closely resemble. Are you an "independent" who likes to do things your own way? Do you need the reinforcement that comes from getting individual approval for your work? Do you dislike sharing blame as well as authority? If so, you should approach job sharing cautiously, making sure that you can set up an arrangement which suits your personal needs and working style.

Some job sharing agreements are defined in such a way that each partner is responsible for a distinct and separate set of tasks or projects. In that situation, responsibility and authority clearly belong to one or the other partner. This allows the partners to work more or less independently, to make unilateral decisions in their own areas of responsibility and to reap the rewards they have earned on their own merits. Even so, the partners must always recognize the need for regular communication and for techniques or strategies to ensure that relevant information is shared effectively.

In many cases, however, job sharing means working cooperatively on tasks or projects for which the partners are jointly responsible. One person may pursue the project to a certain point, at which time the other person takes over and continues working along mutually agreed-upon lines.

Some jobs will lend themselves to either arrangement, but most will be best suited to one or the other. If you have a choice, you can decide on an arrangement that suits your personal style and look for a partner whose needs and style of working are compatible with your own. However, if you are an "independent," and your job does not lend itself to clear divisions of responsibility and authority, you should probably reconsider the whole issue of job sharing.

WORK HABITS

Although some jobs are easier to share than others, the more important consideration is often not the job itself, but whether or not the partners are temperamentally suited to the challenge of making the arrangement work. Here are some of the factors that influence the success of job sharing partners.

- *Flexibility*

Flexibility is at the top of the list of qualities essential for job sharers. Job sharers must be willing to accommodate their work habits and point of view to those of their partner. If you like to "run the show" and are not prepared to negotiate over differences with your partner, job sharing could prove difficult.

- *Organization*

Job sharing cannot work without good organization. The ability to plan ahead and work within an orderly system of procedures is essential. Do you have the necessary organizational skills to make job sharing successful? Do you put files away when you're done with them? If you dislike planning ahead and work best in the midst of a pile of rubble, you may find job sharing incompatible with your style of organization.

- *Collaboration*

Job sharing requires an ability to collaborate on making decisions, assigning tasks and evaluating outcomes. You may have to complete projects or tasks you did not initiate or let your partner take over responsibility for tasks you would prefer to do yourself. Try to assess whether or not you feel comfortable consulting with others and taking advice rather than doing the job "your own way."

- *Communication*

The success of job sharing depends on open and honest communication. A job sharing partnership must be a close working relationship between people who are prepared to deal frankly with each other's needs and opinions. You are likely to run into problems if you find it difficult to say "no" or to criticize another's work.

Would Job Sharing Work in Your Job?

Most jobs can be shared if the partners are committed and compatible. Supervisory positions can be more difficult to share than other jobs; however, there are many examples – a head nurse, a college president and the executive director of a social service agency, for example – of supervisory personnel who have successfully shared their jobs.

So far, most job sharers have been women employed in white-collar professional jobs, largely because these employees are more likely to enjoy a financial position which allows them the freedom to work less. However, job sharing is often equally practical in other kinds of positions. Though the numbers are smaller, successful examples of job sharing can be found within most occupational areas.

It is usually necessary to go through the process of designing and proposing a job sharing arrangement in order to know definitely whether or not it will work in any particular job. See Step Five for detailed instructions on designing a job sharing program.

Spotlight on Job Sharing/Permanent Part-Time

When Dr. Olga Dudek started to practice in Victoria seven years ago, she was the city's only female dentist. Dr. Dudek has recently set another precedent. She is the first dentist in Victoria to split a practice.

Even when she was in dental school, Dr. Dudek knew that she wanted to practice half-time so that she could raise a family. Luckily, she found a willing and compatible partner in Dr. Trudy Rey. In the beginning, the two dentists decided to experiment with the arrangement for three months. Once it appeared the partnership was going to work, they went on to sort out practical details of scheduling and staffing.

Both dentists have separate case loads, except for patients who need emergency treatment, and the office is open six days a week. Each partner works three of the days. They also rotate days every four weeks so that both partners work two Saturdays every month and have two full weekends off. This arrangement accommodates patients who can only make appointments on certain days of the week, especially Saturdays.

Each dentist has her own staff who rotate their days according to her schedule, but there is some overlap for those who want to work four days a week. The dentists and their staff communicate mainly by leaving notes for each other at the end of each rotation. In addition, Dr. Rey and Dr. Dudek meet for lunch once a month. They also organize frequent potluck dinners that give all the staff members a chance to socialize and discuss their work. Because some members of the two staffs are in the office on the same days, they can work together to organize jobs relating to housekeeping, equipment maintenance and the ordering of supplies.

Dr. Dudek is convinced that sharing her practice has significantly reduced the stress commonly associated with dentistry: notably cramped working quarters and nervous patients. She also believes that her income wouldn't be much higher working full-time; higher overheads and income tax would probably offset additional earnings.

With two young children now and a house under construction, Dr. Dudek thinks working full-time would be impossible. Job sharing also gives both partners the flexibility to take long leaves. Recently, Dr. Rey took three months off to travel while Dr. Dudek covered for her. In Dr. Dudek's words "most people have to wait until retirement to realize such a dream, but a partnership makes it possible at a much earlier stage of life."

Permanent Part-Time

Permanent part-time work is less-than-full-time work that:

- pays hourly rates of pay equal to full-time.
- provides full seniority rights, based on a reduced number of hours.
- includes a benefit package that represents a prorated portion of full-time benefits.
- assumes that the employee is a committed and permanent member of the work place team, with full access to further training and career advancement opportunities.

Today, permanent part-time is one of the most flexible and widespread work options. Because it is such a familiar feature in the work place, permanent part-time often meets with less resistance from unions and employers than some of the lesser-known options.

Work schedules can vary from a few days a month or a few weeks of the year to regular half-days or a regular four-and-a-half-day week, and everything in between. The most popular schedules appear to be two- or three-day weeks at eight hours a day or five days a week at four to six hours a day.

Permanent part-time, sometimes called career part-time, has been around for many years. Initially, employers made part-time employment an "exception" for valued employees of long standing who wanted to work less for health or personal reasons. In some cases, the employer would agree to a part-time arrangement simply because the person was too hard to replace. In some fields, particularly female-dominated occupations such as teaching or nursing, well-qualified white-collar professionals have had reasonable success in creating permanent part-time arrangements.

Other occupational areas vary widely in the degree to which permanent part-time work is available. In most large organizations, a few people will be on permanent part-time, even if the option is not generally available. Some industries make heavy use of permanent part-time: within the unionized supermarket industry, for instance, permanent part-time is both widely available and well paid. Some organizations approve of permanent part-time in theory but severely restrict it in practice; the Canadian government has been notorious in this regard. In male-dominated fields such as logging and mining, permanent part-time is so rare that few companies have established personnel policies to cover it.

The treatment accorded to permanent part-time workers also varies greatly. In some teaching and nursing contracts, workers on permanent part-time get full benefits rather than prorated benefits. (In a number of cases, making full benefit packages available to part-time workers has backfired: although a few part-time workers get excellent benefits, management often severely restricts access to permanent part-time because of the increased costs.) In the majority of permanent part-time arrangements, however, employees get benefits proportional to their hours of work. In many cases, the shape of the benefit package is uneven: a permanent employee who works half-time frequently receives full medical and dental coverage but no pension benefit; others may get full pension benefits but have to pay their own medical and dental plan premiums.

People who work half-time or more usually get the best deal on benefits. For persons working less than half-time, rights and benefits may be so minimal that the distinction between "permanent part-time" and "casual part-time" is virtually meaningless.

What Do Employers Think of Permanent Part-Time Work?

Thirty years ago, the vast majority of the work force was made up of full-time workers: predominantly married men with wives at home or young singles of both sexes. The only part-time work available was casual employment at the lowest occupational levels.

Employers viewed part-timers as a casual or peripheral part of the work force. A lot of part-time work was set up for teen-age students. For the employer, hiring students was a cheap way to deal with peak periods or to get the "Joe jobs" done. For the student, part-time jobs provided work experience and some pocket money, but they weren't the main source of support. During the 1950s and 60s, employers developed a number of basic assumptions about part-time work.

- Part-time workers were peripheral, casual, expendable.
- Part-time workers were not supporting themselves, so it didn't matter how little they earned or whether they had job security.
- Part-time workers were under the financial umbrella of their parents or their spouse, so they didn't need any benefits.

- Work was not the main focus of a part-time worker's life, so the employer couldn't expect a long-term commitment or a professional attitude from part-time staff.
- Part-timers were only around on a temporary basis, so it didn't make sense to provide them with training or opportunities for advancement.

Today, many employers consciously or unconsciously see part-time employment in terms of these same basic assumptions. Sometimes this perception is deliberate and self-serving on the part of the employer: it saves the employer a lot of money to pretend that part-time workers deserve less consideration than full-time employees.

As often as not, however, employers have simply failed to notice that the nature of part-time work has changed, because the change has occurred gradually over many years. Nothing has happened to make employers aware that today's part-time worker is "a different animal." In fact, however, the part-time worker of the 1980s and 90s is very different indeed from the "traditional" part-time worker of thirty years ago. Today's permanent part-time workers are:

- working to provide basic family income, not pin money or pocket money.
- committed professionals who work as hard as any other employee.
- self-supporting adults with as much need for job security and employee benefits as any other employee.
- highly productive in both work and non-work activities because they are not spread too thin or operating beyond their limits.
- permanent members of the labour force and consequently a good investment for ongoing training and career development.

As an adult who wants to work less than full-time, your task is to make your employer and your co-workers recognize the difference between you as a permanent part-time employee and the casual part-time worker of the past. Using the term "permanent part-time" is a way to remind your employer that you are not a teenager working for pocket money. It's a way to establish a new concept in your boss's mind that differentiates between the kind of employee you are and out-dated assumptions about part-time workers.

By calling yourself a permanent part-time employee, you may accomplish a lot — or nothing. If your employer simply pastes "permanent part-time" over the mental file that used to say "part-time," nothing will

Spotlight on Permanent Part-Time

Jackie DeRoo is the manager of corporate planning for The Bentall Group, a large construction and real estate development firm based in Vancouver. She manages the system the company uses to prepare budgets and develop strategic and operational plans.

Before going on maternity leave to have her second child, Jackie asked permission to reduce her full-time position to an average of three-fifths time. She also wanted to do more of her work from home.

In her proposal, Jackie described how some of her functions could be delegated to other staff. She also described what new arrangements would be needed in the areas of support staff, salary, benefits and the method of recording her hours. She assessed the costs of installing home telecommuting equipment and also included a detailed timetable to show how her hours would fit in with the varying demands of the planning process.

Because Jackie's supervisor considered her to be a highly-valued member of the management staff, he accepted the proposal for a minimum two-year period. He agreed that the nature of her planning responsibilities was ideally suited to working part-time according to a prearranged schedule that would allow regular staff meetings. Although the company pension plan had no category for permanent part-time employees, the Pension Committee approved Jackie's request for the company to continue its contributions on a prorated basis. The company also agreed to prorate her extensive benefits package.

On the whole, Jackie's new arrangement has worked well on all fronts. Her new secretary also works three-fifths time, and she is happy with this schedule because her husband works shifts and she can spend more time with him. Jackie's supervisor says she is just as effective in her job as she used to be, and he has no doubts about her continued commitment to her work.

So far, the arrangement has had only one drawback. Because of some unique extra planning demands that no one foresaw, Jackie actually worked closer to four-fifths time during her first year on part-time, but she expects to be able to reduce her work hours to the level she prefers. Because Jackie's arrangement has been so successful, her supervisor says the company will probably be prepared to approve other part-time proposals if similar circumstances arise.

change. If, on the other hand, you can persuade your boss to open up a brand new mental file called "permanent part-time" and then begin to fill that file with information about who you are, what your needs are and what your contribution to the workplace could be, it can make a world of difference to the way you are treated. A well-written and persuasive proposal for permanent part-time status can often be the key factor in shifting your employer's attitude.

This difference in thinking stands to benefit both you and your employer. Treating you like a casual worker may cost your employer less in wages and benefits, but it often means that you are underutilized in terms of your potential contribution to the organization. The category of "permanent part-time" has grown rapidly over the last ten years in part because an increasing number of managers have woken up to the fact that some of their most valuable employees do not want to work full-time. Permanent part-time positions have also become increasingly necessary as a way for employers to cover peak periods or offer extended hours.

What Do Unions Think of Permanent Part-Time Work?

Your employer may not be the only one with out-dated ideas about part-time work. Many union executives (particularly male-dominated ones) still think of part-time workers as "teenagers and dilettante housewives who are stealing jobs from real workers." Unions with such anachronistic attitudes often deny membership to part-time workers and do almost nothing to improve the conditions of the part-time work force. These same unions will then point to the bad treatment accorded part-time workers as reasons for fighting tooth and nail against any expansion of part-time employment.

If you happen to be one of those unfortunate Canadians with a union that has its head in the sand where part-time work is concerned, you may be able to help change your union's attitudes by insisting on a clear distinction between traditional part-time and permanent part-time employment.

In addition, you can point to the benefits that progressive, responsive unions have achieved by using the permanent part-time concept. Critics of part-time employment often use the retail sector as a example of how badly part-time workers are exploited. Yet if you are a unionized permanent part-time supermarket clerk in the United Food and Commercial Worker's Union (UFCW), you enjoy good wages, an extensive benefit package and seniority rights. The UFCW doesn't fear the expansion of part-time employment because it has fought hard for fair treatment of its permanent part-time members.

Would Permanent Part-Time Suit Your Needs?

Because so many different schedules are possible, most people can find a variation of permanent part-time that suits their needs. However, people often fail to anticipate some of the hidden factors that can create problems. Consider the following questions carefully before you decide to switch from full-time to part-time.

- *Are you prepared for the possibility of negative reactions from co-workers and supervisors?*

Work places vary a great deal in their ability to tolerate differences. In some settings, co-workers and supervisors will see your part-time status as a positive sign of creativity, flexibility and innovation within the organization. In other companies, however, they may resent you.

You may sense that co-workers and supervisors think you're not serious about your career. When an opportunity for promotion comes up, you could be passed over. Although you may eventually establish your credibility through good job performance, in the short term you might have to accept loss of status and promotion opportunities as a necessary cost of working less.

Your wage and benefit package is a good indicator of your employer's attitude to permanent part-time. If you are getting fair treatment on the economic front, you are less likely to encounter prejudice in other areas. However, if your employer expects you to take a cut in your hourly wage or give up a disproportionate share of benefits, you can probably expect to be treated as a second-class citizen in other ways as well.

- *Are you prepared to let others take over some aspects of your job?*

Working fewer hours almost always means giving up some control over your job. It may mean letting go of tasks that you find rewarding. If you're not around when a last-minute decision comes up, you won't be consulted. You'll also miss out on some news and office gossip. If you enjoy being at the centre of things, you may have to deal with the feeling of being an outsider.

- *Are you prepared to accept a schedule that allows you to meet the demands of your job?*

Some jobs offer limited opportunities for a change in working hours. You may be able to get the amount of time off you want only if you take it at times that suit the needs of your particular job.

- *How will working part-time affect your pension?*

If you have several years of full-time service invested in a pension plan, working part-time could be a costly option in terms of lost income at retirement. This is especially true if you shift to part-time in the years immediately before you retire.

Make sure you have protected your pension before cutting your hours of work. Pensions benefits can always be protected, and most employers are willing to make the necessary arrangements. If not, however, working part-time could wreck your plans for a secure retirement.

Would Permanent Part-Time Work in Your Job?

Many jobs are relatively self-contained. Shift nurses, switchboard operators, assembly-line workers, hotel clerks and air traffic controllers all have well-defined duties that fit into prearranged blocks of time. Because continuity is not a big factor in these jobs, they are relatively easy to adapt to permanent part-time.

Workers who organize their tasks into separate projects or cases are also good candidates for permanent part-time. Some examples are social workers, lawyers, hairdressers, chiropractors, architects and police duty officers. They can usually reduce or redistribute their hours of work by limiting the number of projects or clients they take on.

In jobs that involve a lot of continuity, part-time work may cause disruption within the rest of the organization. People who supervise or coordinate the activities of full-time workers, serve as resources for current information or act as human message boards will find a part-time schedule difficult to manage. Small cuts in work time (a four-day week, for example) may be feasible if good communication mechanisms are part of the program. For larger reductions in work time, job sharing is a better choice for people in supervisory positions or jobs that centre on the transfer of information.

Leaves of Absence

A leave of absence is a period away from work without loss of employment rights. Reasons for taking a leave include family problems, mental health breaks, further schooling, community service or extended vacations. Leave may be paid or unpaid, depending on the circumstances and the employer. The employer may continue to pay for fringe benefits, but not always.

Leaves of absence are ideal for taking a number of days, weeks or months off work on a one-time basis. For time off on a recurring basis — one month out of every six months, for example — the V-Time option might be a better alternative. Job sharing arrangements can sometimes accommodate the need to be away from work for extended periods of up to six or eight months out of every year.

Leaves of absence fall into two categories: compensatory benefits and discretionary leave. Compensatory leaves include sick leave, parental leave (for the care of sick children), compassionate or bereavement leave, vacations, statutory holidays, maternity leave and, in some work places, paternity leave for the fathers of newborn children and adoption leave for the parents of newly adopted children.

Compensatory leaves are rights of employment; they are available to all employees in a given work place. Compensatory leaves are almost always the product of negotiations between employers and the union or employee association. Individuals have little power to affect them. (For more information, see "Compensatory Benefit Leaves" in Special Cases/ Further Resources.)

Rights to compensatory leave are spelled out in written personnel guidelines or in collective agreements. If you aren't sure what your rights are, ask your personnel department or union representative. You may be surprised to discover that your employer's personnel guidelines cover some compensatory leaves that are not widely known.

Work options usually come under the category of discretionary leave. This kind of leave is a not a right of employment. Management grants permission for discretionary leave on a case-by-case basis. Discretionary leaves include personal leave, extended leave, educational leave, "time-buyer" plans and sabbatical leaves.

Types of Leave

Before making a request for a leave of absence, it's important to consider the various types of leave available as well as their possible consequences.

PERSONAL LEAVE

Personal leave, also known as "leave without pay," "temporary leave," "leave of absence" or simply "leave," is any time away from work that is not covered under other leave programs.

Whether you want time off to climb in the Andes, have a face lift or hair transplant, enroll in a three-month acting course, take your children to Disneyland for a week or stay at home and drink beer in your back yard, you're talking about personal leave. If your work place has no specific policies for illness, bereavement, paternity or adoption leave, you will have to negotiate time off for these purposes within the catch-all framework of personal leave.

Personal leave is almost always leave without pay: that's the bad news. The good news is that you can structure a personal leave to fit your individual needs. Because there's no paycheque attached, personal leave is not a "benefit." This means your request doesn't need to qualify under a company-wide program, nor does it set a precedent for other employees.

Although personal leave is usually unpaid, many work places allow employees to go on receiving benefits while on leave. Benefits frequently continue for up to 90 days, but they may go on longer if the leave is granted for health or educational reasons. Leaves which last longer than 90 days are usually handled under provisions for extended leave.

In a few cases, personal leave may be included as an employee benefit (meaning that management must approve a request if the employee gives appropriate notice), though management can sometimes refuse a request on the basis of operational considerations. Inconsiderate employees can abuse the right to demand personal leave, and inflexible supervisors can abuse the right to deny it. Some programs try to steer a middle course by giving supervisors authority over requests for personal leave while at the same time either appointing an "umpire" to negotiate disagreements or submitting them to the grievance process.

EXTENDED LEAVE

Most large organizations have extended leave policies that pay neither wages nor benefits but guarantee employees a job when they return to work after an arranged absence of several months or a year. Extended leaves have a variety of names, including "indefinite leave," "inactive status," "leave without pay" or "care and nurturing leave."

Seniority rights are usually suspended during extended leave, and pension arrangements are put "on hold": the employee stays on the pension plan but does not accrue any additional years of service while on leave. Some organizations will allow employees to self-pay employment benefits while on extended leave.

Although extended leave policies guarantee that employees will have a job when they return, it may not be the same job they had before they went on leave. Employees on leave may be required to give notice of their intent to return. (The required period of notice is frequently 90 days.)

For the employer, extended leave policies are relatively inexpensive; costs are limited to finding and training a replacement. However, the ability to take an extended leave without pay can be invaluable for the person who needs a long period of time off work to care for young children or infirm relatives, to take additional training, to travel the world or to engage in missionary service. For this reason, it is worthwhile to include provisions for extended leave in collective agreements or personnel policy manuals.

EDUCATIONAL LEAVE

Educational leave comes in all shapes and sizes, depending on the policy of the employer. It can be paid or unpaid, and it may or may not include continued benefits. Sometimes educational leave is offered as an employee benefit with well-defined eligibility requirements, but it may also be available strictly at the discretion of management. In some cases, employees are allowed to count the time spent attending approved courses as though it were time at work.

Educational leave is seldom treated as a separate program on its own. More often, it shows up as a codicil in other programs such as training or orientation. The personnel policy manual may, for example, define certain short courses or classes (Emergency First Aid, Safety Procedures Update, etc.) as part of an employee's standard duties.

Permission to attend courses or educational programs that are only marginally job-related is often covered in the guidelines for personal leave. Leave for the purpose of attending courses that are not job-related may be included in the extended leave guidelines. Leave to attend school for longer periods while on the company payroll (six-18 months) are usually included in the guidelines for sabbaticals. Some organizations will help employees self-fund an educational leave by facilitating their participation in time-buyer plans.

TIME-BUYER PLANS

Time-buyer plans allow employees to defer part of their income to a later date so that they can self-fund a sabbatical. Time-buyer plans have been available in the teaching field for many years under "five-for-four" or "deferred salary" plans which received special treatment from Revenue Canada.

In a typical five-for-four plan, a teacher would work full-time at 80 per cent of salary for four years and then take the fifth year off on the deferred earnings plus interest. Deferred earnings held in trust by the employer or kept in a separate trust account are not taxed until received by the employee.

Revenue Canada has recently changed its guidelines to extend the rules governing deferred salary plans for teachers to all employees. A useful guide to deferred salary plans in Canada is *The Time Buyer* by Don Abrams (Toronto: Deneau Publishers, 1986).

SABBATICALS

Sabbaticals are paid leaves granted for the purpose of education, research, community service or a "mental health break." Within the university and college communities, professors can usually claim a year's sabbatical leave at half or three-quarters salary after every six years' of full-time teaching. Most academics use their sabbaticals to write or do research, though some may use the time to study for an advanced degree.

Several major Canadian and U.S. corporations make social service sabbaticals available to selected employees. For example, an IBM executive may remain on the company payroll for several months while directing the local United Way fund on a full-time basis. In some high-stress professions (parole officers, for instance) paid sabbaticals lasting a couple of months may be offered every few years as a way of avoiding "burnout."

Spotlight on Leaves of Absence

Rudy Van der Vegt is a teacher in the Greater Nanaimo School District who runs an alternate school for Native Indian teenagers. In addition to teaching all subjects, he is responsible for the practical operation of the program — "from transportation to cooking breakfast occasionally."

Four years ago, the Nanaimo School Board offered all senior teachers in the district a year's leave of absence and approximately $8,000 in lieu of their regular salary. This generous offer was part of an innovative scheme to reduce costs and prevent layoffs of new teachers during an unusually tight fiscal year.

Rudy decided to take advantage of the offer, and with the help of their savings, he and his wife and daughter travelled for a year in Asia. Because their living expenses were low, they actually spent less that year than they would have if they had remained at home.

Rudy and his family enjoyed the experience so much that when he returned to work, Rudy decided to participate in the Deferred Salary Leave Plan available to all teachers in the district. Under this plan, a teacher agrees to defer a fixed percentage of salary for a certain number of years. The school district holds the money in trust and invests it in a specified financial institution. During the period of leave, the teacher receives payments from the plan instead of a regular salary. The plan also pays for sick leave credits, superannuation deductions and premiums for fringe benefits.

During the first year, Rudy decided to defer one-third of his salary, but that was too difficult to manage, so for the second and third year, he is taking three-quarters of his salary. At the end of the third year, he will be able to draw 80 per cent of his present salary which he will use to take his family on another trip to Asia. The school district won't guarantee him the same job when he returns, but he will be offered a position in the same salary range somewhere in the district. This is a chance he is prepared to take, although he is pretty sure he will be able to get his present job back as he did after the previous leave.

Rudy calls the plan a form of "enforced savings." When he returns from his Asian expedition, he plans to contract for his third leave.

Employers rarely grant sabbaticals unless they foresee some benefit to themselves as a result in terms of good public relations for the organization or an improvement in the health or professional stature of the employee.

Would a Leave of Absence Suit Your Needs?

The conditions surrounding leaves of absence vary a great deal, depending on the type of leave, the policies of the employer and the terms of any collective agreement. Different kinds of leave have significantly different effects on income, benefits, seniority and the right to return to the same job.

In each of these areas, it is important to establish both what you want and also what you would accept. In your proposal you can ask for what you want; if that's granted, everything is wonderful. If your employer will only give you part of what you want, you'll need to be clear on what's feasible for you — and what isn't.

INCOME

Can you make a good case for a paid leave? Educational leave for work-related schooling may be either fully or partly paid. If you take a leave of absence to head up the local United Way campaign, it's good publicity for your employer, and you can use that argument to justify staying on the company payroll. Leaves associated with family responsibilities are sometimes negotiated into collective agreements. Consider whether you can afford to take unpaid leave if that is all that is available.

BENEFITS

Some leave arrangements come with full fringe benefits, whereas others require that you cover the cost of your benefits while you are off work. Many collective agreements make provisions for benefits to be covered during short-term leaves, but longer leaves may not be covered. Again, consider whether you could afford the time off work if it involved covering the cost of your fringe benefits out of your own pocket.

SENIORITY

Depending on your particular agreement, you may or may not accrue seniority while you're off work. If you do not accrue seniority, how many people will pass you on the seniority list, and will this have any affect on your job security or your duty assignment? Most people on leave continue to accrue seniority, but if that's not available to you, would you still want to go ahead?

RIGHT TO RETURN

You may not be guaranteed the right to return to the same position, particularly if you take an open-ended leave. Consider how important this factor is to you. If you feel that it's essential to keep your present position, you may want to make your leave proposal contingent upon being able to resume your current duties.

Would a Leave of Absence Work in Your Job?

The answer to this question depends on whether or not you can make satisfactory arrangements to ensure that your work gets done while you're gone. This might require finding a temporary replacement or arranging to delay your work until you return.

Think about your job in light of the considerations raised in the previous discussions of job sharing and permanent part-time. Also consider the following questions.

- *Do you have unique skills or characteristics that are essential to the performance of your duties?*

This could include a diverse contact network, long-established client relationships or, in the case of a graphic artist, a distinctive artistic style.

- *Are you involved in a project (or projects) that would make it difficult for you to turn your responsibilities over to someone else? Would the person taking over for you require a long period of training and orientation?*

If the answer to one or more of these questions is "yes," your employer will probably resist a request for a leave. However, that's not necessarily a reason for giving up.

- *If you were in an accident or became seriously ill and needed to be away from work for several weeks or months, how would your employer cope? Would a fellow worker or a part-time employee take over your responsibilities temporarily? Would several people share your duties? Would your employer advertise for someone to fill a temporary position? Would your work be "put on hold" until you returned?*

No one is indispensable. If you were away on sick leave for an extended period, your employer would have to find a way to deal with the situation. Granting your request for a leave may be difficult, but it's unlikely to be impossible. Besides, if you are really "irreplaceable" in your job, your employer should be interested in keeping you healthy and satisfied, even if that means doing without you for awhile.

V-Time

In 1976, the Santa Clara County Employees Union in California conducted a survey of employee needs. Among other things, the survey revealed that a significant number of workers wanted to reduce their hours — even if it meant a corresponding loss of income. However, the pattern of responses was not uniform. Some employees wanted no change in their work time. Among those who wanted to work less, needs varied both in terms of the the amount of time they wanted to work and when.

In response to this survey, the union developed a proposal for a new work schedule called V-Time (short for "voluntary reduced work time"). The program established rules for a time/income trade off which would give employees a range of choices for reducing their hours (and their income) by a fixed percentage over a set period of time.

Management initially vetoed the concept. Then in 1980, the passage of Proposition 13 resulted in lower property taxes, and the municipality was faced with the need to trim its budget. As an alternative to laying off employees, management agreed to experiment with V-Time.

Individual employees, the union and management all benefited from the program; and in the years since, V-Time has spread to numerous state and local governments. New York State recently instituted a pilot program, and the Province of Quebec is working to promote V-Time in both the public and private sectors. The key elements of a V-Time program are:

a variety of time-off choices defined as a percentage of full-time. Some programs have as many as 12 possible options. In a fairly typical program, the range of choices would be 2.5, 5, 10, 20, 25 and 40 per cent of full-time.

a choice of time off in the form of a shorter work day, a shorter work week or extended vacation time. The table below illustrates a sample range of options, assuming a 40-hour week as the baseline.

income prorated in direct proportion to hours worked. Employees retain benefits, although some may be prorated, particularly for large reductions in work time.

approval by the employee's immediate supervisor required for participation in the program and the form of time-off. Most programs have an appeals process or an umpire to help employees and supervisors reach agreement.

periodic opportunities for enrollment and renewal. These usually occur every three, six or twelve months although some programs are continuously open for applications.

Sample Range of V-Time Options

A pay reduction of	hours off per day	days off per month	weeks off per year
means	or		or
2.5%	12 minutes	.5	1.25
5%	25 minutes	1	2.5
10%	45 minutes	2	5
20%	1.5 hours	4	10
25%	2 hours	5	12.5
40%	3.25 hours	8	20

Employers often resist V-Time proposals initially, but if they can be persuaded to offer the program on a temporary or trial basis, their resistance often turns quickly to support. They discover that V-Time is an inexpensive way to improve employee morale and reduce burnout. This, in turn, increases productivity and reduces absenteeism and turnover.

V-Time can be a way to keep valued employees who might leave because they are under too much pressure. For companies in a difficult financial situation, it can be a creative alternative to layoffs by spreading the available work around. Why force people out onto the street when some employees would prefer to work less?

Would V-Time Suit Your Needs?

V-Time programs are popular with employees because they allow more time off without a huge loss of income. Pay cuts are usually in a range that most people can afford, whereas job sharing or permanent part-time usually mean a substantial drop in pay. Although the amount of free time gained is moderate, V-Time is also flexible enough to meet a wide range of needs.

Spotlight on V-Time

David Parsons and Jacalyn Hamilton are environmental planners with the B.C. Ministry of the Environment. Their work involves assessing the environmental impact of proposed commercial and industrial projects and designing plans to safeguard the environment.

David Parsons also owns a farm, and V-Time lets him take every Friday off so that he and his family can spend more time there. David says his V-Time schedule is "delightful because it allows me to do things that are important to me outside the job."

Jacalyn Hamilton cares passionately about both her work and her children, and V-Time lets her feel good about both. "I would have great difficulty working at all," she says, "if this option were not available."

The V-Time program at the Ministry of the Environment has been in operation since 1983. At that time, the department was facing the prospect of layoffs, and one employee was about to lose his job. Some of his co-workers offered to work less so that the department would have enough money to provide another salary. Since the program started, six employees have elected to shorten their work week by between 10 and 40 per cent. However, they can always return to full-time if they give 20 days notice. Participants get full medical and dental coverage, and most other benefits are prorated, including sick leave and holiday pay.

V-Time is no longer necessary in order to avoid layoffs, but the program has been continued by popular demand. Now the money that the department saves from V-Time goes into hiring short-term contract staff to deal with special projects and prevent backlogs. This option gives management some useful staffing flexibility.

Everyone agrees that V-Time has resulted in a "great improvement in staff morale." In the opinion of Branch Manager John Dick, "The V-Time participants have been some of the most productive employees." He thinks the program has either "maintained or enhanced" their productivity. Problems with the program have been minor. The branch manager and the payroll clerk both have to do some extra work to accommodate the non standard schedules, and one participant found that a V-Time schedule requires flexible day care arrangements.

However, Jacalyn Hamilton is satisfied with her schedule, and David Parsons says, "Without reduced hours, I was always squeezing things, always on a treadmill. I'm a much happier person now."

Parents of preschool or school age children often choose the option of a shorter work day. For others, an extra day off a month or a few extra weeks of vacation can make the difference between surviving and burning out. Because golf courses, riding stables, tennis courts and other recreational facilities tend to be less crowded in the middle of the week, a midweek afternoon can be an ideal time for a break from the office.

V-Time is appropriate for anyone who wants a small cut in working hours (from two per cent to 40 per cent) on an ongoing basis. V-Time also allows individual employees to choose different schedules for their time off. This feature accommodates a wide range of uses for free time, from parenting and further education to volunteer work, recreation and travel. V-Time programs usually include the option of returning to full-time at the end of any twelve-month period. This is an important protection in case you need to go back to full-time for financial reasons.

V-Time has one important limitation: it is a payroll and personnel system for a group of employees. It is not an option for one individual within a department or organization. However, an individual employee can achieve the same result by negotiating an arrangement for permanent part-time.

Setting up a V-Time program is a lot of work, but if several employees want to reduce their hours, a collective proposal for V-Time would be easier than each person making a separate proposal for part-time. A group proposal would also simplify management's task. If you think you would have difficulty getting your employer's agreement to permanent part-time, making a group V-Time proposal might increase your chances of success.

V-Time is often attractive to unions because it makes work options available to all employees on equal terms. At the same time, it allows room for individual needs and differences. Your union may be willing to help design a collective V-Time program. The support of a strong union can make a big difference in discussions with your employer.

In addition to giving workers greater flexibility, V-Time can also play an important role as a creative alternative to layoffs. When an employer threatens layoffs, it often turns out that a lot of people would be willing to work less rather than lose a number of full-time positions. A carefully designed V-Time proposal from a group of employees can often convince management that there is a viable alternative to putting people out of work. (See Step Six for more information about avoiding layoffs.)

Would V-Time Work in Your Job?

In deciding whether V-Time would fit your situation, the questions to answer are the same as for permanent part-time.

- *What effects will your temporary absence have on the job you have to do?*

- *What will happen to your work when you are away?*

- *How can you minimize disruption for others?*

Because the cuts in work time are usually small, V-Time adapts well to most jobs. In fact, if you often get sick because you are overloaded and burned out, going on V-Time may even help you get more work done.

However, if you are planning to cut your work time by more than five per cent, you'll need to plan on shedding some of your responsibilities or delegating them to others. Having more time off won't do you much good if it means overloading yourself during working hours.

Banked Overtime

For many Canadians, mandatory overtime is a burden — the difference between a manageable workload and an unmanageable one. As one exhausted employee put it, "I'm sick and tired of feeling sick and tired." Banked overtime doesn't eliminate this problem. However, it's usually easier to get than a ban on overtime.

Banked overtime gives workers the right to take paid time off as compensation for working extra hours. The idea of banked overtime is not new. It has been around for years, both formally as organized programs and informally as a matter of mutual consent between employees and employers.

Formal programs with adequate relief staffing are generally effective at compensating employees adequately. Informal arrangements are often less successful. In many cases, banked overtime exists only on paper: employees are entitled to compensatory time off, but in practice they never get it because it's never "convenient" for the employer.

Well-organized programs avoid this problem by hiring full-time relief staff to fill in for employees who are taking compensatory time off. Employees book their compensatory time according to the availability of relief staff. In order to even out the pressure on replacement staff, firms with known peak periods often allow anticipatory time off (workers use their compensatory time off before they've earned it). Good systems also have an overtime umpire and a committee to deal with grievances.

Would Banked Overtime Suit Your Needs?

Banked overtime can be useful if you don't want to work more than 40 hours but at the same time, you don't care too much when you put in your time. Banked overtime is even more attractive if, for personal reasons, you would prefer to work weekends and have more free time during the week.

If you like to golf or ski, time off during the week might be ideal. You might prefer to work on Sunday when the golf links and ski slopes are crowded and then take Thursday or Friday off so you can golf or ski without lining up. If you like to camp or fish, you may be able to exchange weekend work for additional vacation time.

HOW DO YOU FEEL ABOUT BANKED OVERTIME...?

On the other hand, if it's important to keep your work from interfering with your weekends and evenings, you won't be satisfied with banked overtime. The only solution for you would be either a ban on mandatory overtime or the addition of a weekend relief shift at your work place. At one of its Ontario plants, for example, 3M Corporation employs a weekend shift that works 12 hours Saturday and 12 hours Sunday and gets paid for 40 hours. The arrangement keeps the plant open seven days a week, avoids overtime and is popular with both the weekday and the weekend shifts.

If you are used to working overtime and getting paid for it, you may have grown accustomed to the extra income. In that case, banked overtime may not have much appeal. If you're not sure how banked overtime would affect your finances, don't skip Step Four. Remember, too, that Revenue Canada takes at least one-quarter of your overtime pay.

Would Banked Overtime Work in Your Job?

The crucial element in a successful banked overtime program is adequate relief staffing. If you are going to start banking your overtime, who will relieve you when you want to take your compensatory time off? How long would it take to train your replacement, and would that person also be able to relieve other employees with similar jobs?

It's obviously easier and more economical for an employer to offer banked overtime if a relief person can cover for several employees. For this reason, banked overtime works best for factory jobs, clerical positions, construction jobs, police work, fire fighting and the medical professions.

If your job is a one-of-a-kind position, banking overtime will be harder to manage. Your replacement would probably require a great deal of training if your work involves a unique talent or skill or if your job is built around on-going relationships (for example, psychotherapy or social work).

If you are on salary, you probably don't get paid for overtime. In that case, you will probably have difficulty negotiating banked overtime with your employer, regardless of the kind of work you do.

In discussions of overtime, many employers have a hidden agenda based on unacknowledged economic benefits (see "The Politics of Overtime"). For this reason, some employers adamantly refuse to ban overtime or hire relief staff to cover peak periods. They may agree to a banked overtime program, but usually reluctantly and sometimes only under strong pressure from a union.

If you want to institute a banked overtime program at your work place, you will probably need the help of your union or a persuasive, well-written

Spotlight on Banked Overtime

David English is a research technician with the Tides and Currents Section of the Canadian Hydrographic Service located at the Institute of Ocean Sciences in Sidney, B.C. He installs and services tide gauges in the western Arctic and then collects and processes the data. During the winter months, he also does undersea diving to retrieve research instruments placed along the Pacific coast.

David spends two to three months every year travelling and doing fieldwork, and this means he builds up considerable overtime. His contract allows him to take his banked overtime either in cash or as compensatory leave. Although the majority of David's male co-workers are married with children, they typically choose to convert their overtime into cash rather than time off. David decided to take a different approach. Because he has to be away so much, he wanted to spend more time at home with his two young daughters during the months when he isn't doing fieldwork. To make this possible, he decided to use his banked overtime to take every Friday off.

One of his daughters goes to preschool, so David takes her to school on Fridays and sometimes does a duty day with the other parents. David's wife works part-time, and the fact that he is home on one of her working days helps to reduce child care expenses. Because he enjoys carpentry, David prefers to do his own house repairs rather than pay someone else to do them. He can use his Fridays off to work on the house, and this leaves the weekend free for family outings.

David's decision to take more time off happened to coincide with a new development in overtime policy within his division. Because overtime payments were exceeding the amount allotted in the budget, staff were requested to take a portion of their overtime in compensatory leave. David's supervisor thinks staff will eventually become used to the idea of taking more leave, and he hopes they will follow David's example. He says that other staff have been able to adjust their workloads to accommodate David's four-day week because it is predictable.

David's wife likes the choice he has made. "It gives the children a chance to be with him all day," she says. "The prospect of spending long weekends together also helps me accept the fieldwork better." David agrees. "Fieldwork can be hard on families," he says. "Compensatory leave is one way that I can do my job and still spend more time with my family."

proposal—unless you are fortunate enough to have an employer who is willing to look at the high human cost of excessive overtime.

The Politics of Overtime

Overtime may or may not mean more money in the weekly paycheque. Either way, however, it has some serious negative consequences for workers, employers and the society at large.

- Workers are under more stress and have less time to spend with their families.
- High levels of overtime result in larger rates of turnover, absenteeism, accidents and health problems.
- High use of overtime translates into high rates of unemployment. The Swedish experience suggests that banked overtime and relief staffing could provide jobs for up to four per cent of the Canadian workforce.

If overtime has such negative consequences, why does it figure so prominently in our economy? Why do so many employers refuse to ban overtime or to hire relief staff to deal with peak periods? Overtime is desirable for a number of reasons.

- It adds greatly to a firms's flexibility in dealing with peak periods, equipment breakdowns and rush orders.
- It permits companies to get more production out of the same overhead.
- Overtime pay is a significant and necessary part of the income of many workers.
- Overtime often helps consumers get goods and services faster.

In addition, there are a couple of hidden economic reasons why employers rely on overtime.

- *Salaried employees often work extra hours without any compensation.*

In many organizations the official work week for salaried employees is 40 hours per week, but the expected work week may be 50 hours or more. Promotions are reserved for "committed" employees (those who put in a lot of extra hours for free).

Because most salaried workers are not unionized, it is difficult to organize against this kind of exploitation. Although provincial labour codes offer some protection (at least on paper), individuals acting alone are vulnerable to being blacklisted within their organizations.

● *Overtime represents a significant savings in the cost of benefits.*

A full benefit package adds roughly 40 per cent to the cost of wages, but benefits are "paid for" in the first 40 hours. There are no additional benefit costs attached to overtime. This means that overtime is, in effect, 40 per cent cheaper than hiring relief workers.

Even if an employer pays a 50 per cent premium for overtime, the 40 per cent savings on benefits makes overtime only slightly more expensive than hiring extra staff. In addition to benefits, extra staff require training and, in some cases, severance pay.

The economics of our payroll structure encourages employers to resort to systematic overtime even though relief staffing or an extra shift would be better personnel policy. These employers seem unaware of the hidden costs of overtime: lost productivity, absenteeism, accidents and staff turnover.

Phased Retirement

Phased retirement is a catch-all name for a variety of programs which enable older workers to reduce their work hours in the years preceding full retirement. Many people experience retirement as a sudden shock or loss of identity and self-worth. Phased retirement programs give older workers time to begin developing new roles, relationships, avocations and interests before they retire.

Sometimes older employees work fewer hours only in the six months before they plan to retire. Sometimes the reduction starts five years before retirement, and sometimes phased retirement lasts 15 to 20 years. Most phased retirement programs include pre-retirement planning courses, some sort of pension protection and training for the retiring employee's successor.

Sometimes phased retirement takes the form of extended vacations, but most people choose to work a shorter week. Reductions in work time vary from 10 per cent to 50 per cent. Sometimes the phasing out of full-time work progresses from a four-day week at age 62 to a three-day week at age 63 and half-time at age 64.

Phased retirement is rapidly becoming the norm in Europe. In Sweden, for instance, any worker over age 60 can collect a partial pension while working half-time. However, phased retirement programs are relatively unknown in Canada as yet. This means that most Canadian workers must initiate their own plans for phased retirement.

Models of Phased Retirement

Phased retirement programs can be designed in several ways; the following are the five most common models.

COMPANY-PAID PROGRAMS

Some companies give workers approaching retirement age extra vacation time or a shorter work week with no loss in pay. Because such programs are expensive to the employer, the benefits tend to be relatively short term (six months to one year). Although this isn't really enough time to prepare for retirement (particularly when time off

Thinking Clearly About Retirement

Most Canadians will spend close to one-third of their adult life in retirement. Whether these are "the best years" or the worst depends in large part on thoughtful preparation and planning. It also depends on how realistically we view this new stage of life.

Most people have some fears about retirement: "I'll feel useless"; "I won't have enough human contact"; "I'll be bored," or "I'll get sick or senile." Many people run away from these fears by throwing themselves wholeheartedly into their work. These people are pretending that they will never retire. For them, retirement often comes as a traumatic and sometimes fatal shock.

Fears about retirement should be seen as inner messages that say "Pay attention. You may have some problems to deal with." Realistic planning for retirement means facing your fears and finding solutions to your concerns. The solutions may involve initiating new relationships, developing new interests and activities or learning how to take better care of your health.

Most people also have fantasies about retirement: "I'll be able to sleep late"; "We'll travel all the time"; "I'll be able to (play golf, go fishing, visit the grandchildren, etc.) whenever I want." These are all ways of saying, "Life may be lousy now, but everything will be wonderful when I retire."

People who fantasize about retirement are likely to be bitterly disappointed. After three months of non-stop travel (or golf or fishing), they feel bored and jaded. Realistic planning for retirement involves testing our fantasies in practice. It means abandoning illusions and acquiring habits and skills that will make our dreams come true.

It's difficult to develop new interests, relationships, activities and skills while working full-time. This is particularly true for men, because men in our society are encouraged to define themselves entirely in terms of their work. For people over the age of 50, phased retirement can be a chance to practice for the real thing.

takes the form of a longer vacation), these programs involve no loss of either income or pension.

EMPLOYEE-PAID PROGRAMS

In this approach, older workers are allowed to reduce their work hours if they agree to take a proportionate cut in salary. Pension contributions are usually based on the full-time salary in order to avoid any effect on the employee's pension after retirement. Although this approach results in a loss of income, it has a number of advantages.

- The arrangement can be designed for individual cases.
- The arrangement permits substantial flexibility in the length of the phasing period and the size of the reduction in work time.
- The arrangement is usually easier to negotiate than other forms of phased retirement because it involves a minimum of expense to the employer.

PARTIAL PENSION SCHEMES

A few Canadian organizations (the University of Alberta, for example) use an approach that is popular in Europe and the United States. Partial pension schemes allow workers past a certain age (usually 55 or 60) to start collecting a small pension to help cover the income lost by working part-time. Under such an arrangement, older employees could work a three-day week (60 per cent time) and still take home 80 to 90 per cent of their regular paycheque. In terms of cost, partial pension schemes are often a satisfactory middle ground for both the employer and the employee.

INTEGRATED OPTION PLANS

With slight modifications, options like V-Time, job sharing, personal leave or permanent part-time can be adapted to provide a phased retirement program. Only two changes are required: courses in pre-retirement planning should be offered to older workers, and the pension plan should be changed to allow contributions based on full-time salary.

POST-RETIREMENT WORK POOLS

Some companies offer retired employees temporary or relief jobs and/or short-term contracts for special projects. This arrangement

Spotlight on Phased Retirement

Ken Waldock is a computer programming analyst who works for Victoria General Hospital in the Management Information Services department. As he approached the age of 65, Ken wanted to reduce his hours from full-time to part-time. He asked for permission to decrease his work time gradually over a two-year period to 22.5 hours per week. Since this arrangement also met the needs of the department, his manager agreed.

At that time, the Management Information Services department was changing over from IBM equipment to a new DEC system, and new staff were being trained to work with the DEC equipment. However, because the information systems in the hospital were being transferred one department at a time, the hospital still needed a programmer with experience on the IBM system. Ken's desire to reduce his hours fitted perfectly with the hospital's plans to phase into a new computer system.

Ken says phased retirement has been a "boon" to him, but he admits his case and circumstances were special; he had been with the hospital for only two and a half years as a casual full-time employee, so he had no pension plan or benefits package. That made negotiations easier.

Because the personnel department at the hospital doesn't recognize phased retirement as a work option, Ken and his manager had to work out a new employee-employer relationship. Instead of keeping him on staff as a part-time employee, the department gave Ken a two-year contract as a computer consultant. For the first year, he worked 30 hours a week and later reduced his schedule to 22.5 hours a week, or 4.5 hours a day. He usually works from 7:30 a.m. to noon every morning, but he can rearrange his hours if he wants to take a long weekend.

For Ken, the major advantages of phased retirement are the continued income and the opportunity for mental stimulation. He also feels more in charge of his own life than he did when he was working full-time. Within his arrangement, he can organize his own hours as long as he fulfills his commitments to his client-departments. If he works more than 22.5 hours per week, he gets paid for it.

Despite the fewer hours, Ken feels just as involved with his work as he did before. However, now that the two years are almost up, he feels more prepared to retire. When there are no longer any departments using the IBM system at the hospital, Ken says that he will take a holiday and then look around for some other part-time opportunities.

gives retired workers extra income and a chance to stay involved for as long as they need or want. Employers often find this approach to relief staffing both cheaper and more effective than using "temps" or consultants.

Would Phased Retirement Suit Your Needs?

Some people use phased retirement as a preparation for full retirement, but for most people the pay-off is more immediate. They are simply enjoying the opportunity for more free time now. By age 50 or 55, many people have paid off the house, and their children have left home. They have less need for a full-time income (or two). Often, people at this age also feel less frantic about the need to prove themselves through work; they are more interested in doing what pleases them. Desires and ambitions that may have been set aside in order to be "responsible" begin to come to the surface. The need to spend more time on family, friends, volunteer commitments, relaxation, hobbies or a second career seems much more urgent.

For many people, phased retirement offers the opportunity to enjoy the kind of balanced life they have always wanted. It's one of the few socially acceptable ways of having a life that isn't dominated by work. However, phased retirement has some drawbacks worth considering.

- *Are you prepared for the possibility you may be taken less seriously on the job?*

Some of your colleagues will envy you because you are working less than they are. Inside they may be thinking, "I wish I had the guts to take some time for myself and my family the way Harry has." But this may come out as something like "Old Harry can't cut the mustard any more. They've already put him out to pasture." In some organizations, your status may actually improve by working less. In others, you may notice subtle or not-so-subtle signs of discrimination.

- *Are you prepared to share some of your duties?*

In a phased retirement program, you will probably be sharing your duties with your successor. That's fine if you get along with that person. If not, the experience could be awkward or downright painful. In that case, you might be wise to make your participation in a phased retirement program contingent on finding an acceptable partner/successor.

● *How much loss of income can you afford?*

In phased retirement, your income could shrink as much as 50 per cent, depending on how much you want to work and the kind of arrangement you negotiate. The more expensive the arrangement is for your employer, the less likely you are to get the deal approved. The trick is to find a middle ground that you and your employer can both afford.

● *How much of your pension can you afford to lose?*

Most phased retirement plans are designed so that your company pension will be the same as if you had worked full-time right up to retirement. In partial pension schemes, however, there is some loss of pension income, usually on the order of five to 10 percent. If your employer can't or won't adjust the pension plan to meet your needs, your pension could conceivably be cut by up to half. It's important to know what your bottom line is for pension income so you can walk away from any phased retirement offer that doesn't measure up.

● *Are you an all-or-nothing person?*

Most people dislike drastic change, but some people thrive on it. If you're the kind of person who handles a crisis better than incremental adjustments, you can probably handle full retirement better than a gradual disengagement.

Would Phased Retirement Work in Your Job?

It's possible to design a phased retirement schedule that will work for almost every job, including management positions. In a few cases, it will be necessary to transfer to a different job in order to be eligible for phased retirement, but this is the exception rather than the rule.

For smaller reductions in work time (five to 30 percent), the criteria are essentially the same as for V-Time. The criteria for job sharing apply to larger cuts in working time.

Flexitime

Flexitime was invented in 1967 by a West German management consultant named Christel Kammerer. She devised the scheme in order to solve a problem that had developed at an aerospace research and development centre near Munich. Lateness and absenteeism had increased because more employees owned cars, and they had started driving to work over poor roads leading to the plant.

Kammerer's flexitime scheme produced the desired improvement in traffic flow, but managers were surprised by the extent of the benefits: absenteeism declined by about 40 per cent, overtime dropped by about 50 per cent, employee turnover was reduced, tardiness disappeared and morale rose sharply.

After that, flexitime spread fairly quickly throughout Europe and eventually made similar progress in the U.S. About 30 per cent of U.S. firms now have part of their work force on flexible hours. Although Canadian estimates are somewhat lower, flexitime is the best known and most widely used work option in Canada.

"Flexitime" and "flexible hours" are generic substitutes for the copyrighted term "Flextime." Like "Xerox" or "Kleenex," the "Flextime" copyright is now so widely ignored as to be almost meaningless. However, "flexitime" is more acceptable from a legal standpoint.

Flexitime refers to flexible working hours. Employees on flexitime work a fixed number of hours every day or week, but they can choose their starting and quitting times. For example, an employee might work eight hours a day by starting at 8 a.m. and finishing at 4 p.m. Another employee in the same department might start at 9:30 a.m. and finish at 5:30 p.m.

Most flexitime schemes use the following terms and concepts:

bandwidth – the period between the earliest starting time and the latest quitting time.

flexible starting time – a period of time within which employees can begin the work day (for example, between 7 a.m. and 10 a.m.).

flexible quitting time – a period of time within which employees can end the work day (for example, between 2 p.m. and 6 p.m.).

Spotlight on Flexitime

   Katherine Rempel is the office administrator for the Victoria branch
of National Life of Canada. She is one of two office staff who provide support services for the branch manager and eight sales representatives.
   Katherine works from 8 a.m. to 4:30 p.m., and her office partner works
from 8:30 a.m. to 5 p.m. They are both taking advantage of a company-
wide Flextime schedule introduced by the head office of National Life in
Toronto. Under the National Life Flextime program, all staff must be on
duty during core hours from 9:30 a.m. to 11:30 p.m. and from 1:30 p.m. to
3:10 p.m. Flexible hours are from 7:15 a.m. to 9:30 a.m. and 3:10 p.m. to
6:15 p.m. In a large city, the company's Flextime program helps staff avoid
the worst of the rush hour. By providing extended office hours, it also
helps the company with the need to conduct business between a number of
time zones. The branch office in Victoria has special needs, however, so its
employees have somewhat less flexibility in the hours they work.
   Because only two people are available to answer phone calls, one person must be in the office early in the morning in order to receive head office calls from Toronto. Someone also has to be in the office after 4:30
p.m. to take local calls. From the company's point of view, it makes good
sense to stagger the hours of the two office staff in Victoria.
   Katherine is satisfied with her hours because she describes herself as a
natural early bird, and even a 7:30 a.m. start is not too early for her. By
finishing her work at 4:30, she can be home by 5 p.m. and have the whole
evening to spend with her family. As a single parent for many years, she
has also been able to cut her child care costs by working an early schedule.
At work, Katherine enjoys at least an hour when she can concentrate
without a lot of interruptions. Since there are no peak periods, she and her
office partner can adjust their lunch hours to suit themselves as long as one
person is always available to answer the phone.
   Flexibility is limited in a small office, but fortunately Katherine
doesn't have to contend with the heavy rush hour traffic of a large city. She
prefers an early schedule, and she is pleased that in her 16 years with insurance companies, that option has always been available.

core time — a time period when all employees must be at work (for example, between 10 a.m. and 2 p.m.).

mid-day flexibility — a mid-day time period during which employees may be away from work (for example, between 11 a.m. and 1 p.m.).

Sample Programs

With mid-day flexibility:

7 a.m.	10 a.m.	noon	2 p.m.	3 p.m.	6 p.m.

flexible starting time	core time	mid-day flexibility	core time	flexible quitting time

Without mid-day flexibility:

7:30 a.m.	10 a.m.	2 p.m.	5:30 p.m.

flexible starting time	core time	flexible quitting time

Flexitime is based on the assumption that employees will work a standard number of hours, and pay periods are also based on this assumption. Some adjustment is necessary when there is a difference between salaried hours and actual hours. These adjustments are made at the end of accounting intervals called "settlement periods." Some systems require employees to adjust their work hours in order to come out even at the end of each settlement period. These are called "zero balance" systems. Other systems allow employees to carry over an excess or deficit of hours from one settlement period to the next.

In systems with no carry-over provision, flexibility increases with the length of the settlement period. If the settlement period were one day, for example, you would have to arrange your starting and quitting times (or your lunch hour) so that you worked the required seven or eight hours each day. If the settlement period lasted four weeks, however, you could work different amounts from day to day and week to week, as long as you

··· YOU WERE ASKING ABOUT FLEXTIME, BRAWNLEY···?

ended the four-week period with the required 140 to 160 hours to your credit.

Accounting is simple in zero balance systems, but they don't have much flexibility for dealing with fluctuating work loads or changes in the responsibilities employees have outside work. Hours banking provides this kind of flexibility. Hours banking means adding or subtracting any surplus or deficit of hours from the employee's "account" in the "hours bank" at the end of each settlement period.

Hours banking can have significant benefits, including extra days off. For example, if you are salaried for 35 hours per week and you work an average of seven and a half hours each day, you would earn one full day off every 14 working days. With hours banking, you could take every third Friday off.

Many systems have rules that ensure adequate front-line coverage. Certain individuals may be designated to cover lunch hour or the beginning or end of the business day. If hours banking is allowed, days off must sometimes be booked in advance on a rota system in order to guarantee essential coverage.

Would Flexitime Suit Your Needs?

Flexitime allows you to change your schedule without any reduction in your hours, your paycheque or your benefits. For many people, especially commuters, this is an attractive option. If you commute to work in the thick of the rush hour, flexitime may help reduce your commuting time.

Other advantages include the ability to tailor your work day to your children's school schedule. If you're an early bird or a night hawk, flexitime can also make a big difference to your comfort and your efficiency on the job. Flexitime with hours banking can satisfy your need for a long weekend every so often if you don't mind working an additional half-hour every day.

If your work involves peaks and valleys, you may spend some of your time struggling to catch up and the rest wondering what to do with yourself. In that case, flexitime can function as an informal version of banked overtime. You can work late when things are hectic and take time off when the work load is light, without any effect on your paycheque.

If your basic problem is overwork, flexitime won't help — unless it drastically reduces commuting time. Many people mistakenly think that flexitime will make their job easier, but that's not the way it works. If you're overloaded or burned out, you should consider a work option that involves working fewer hours.

Would Flexitime Work in Your Job?

Flexitime is not practical for all jobs. If your job requires constant in-teraction with other staff members, you probably need to work the same hours as your co-workers. Flexitime is usually not possible for assembly line workers, for example. However, if you work independently a lot of the time, flexible hours won't present many problems. Most office jobs can be adapted to fit into a flexible schedule.

Flexitime is also appropriate if you have some discretion in the scheduling of your work load. Professionals like social workers, chiropractors and investment counsellors can often book appointments to coincide with a flexible schedule. If you are a member of a "response pool" of telephone operators, sales representatives or shipping clerks, for instance, flexitime will work if it is designed to ensure adequate staff coverage.

If flexitime won't work in your job, you could look at the possibility of V-Time, banked overtime or a compressed work week, particularly one that involves staggered hours.

Compressed and Modified Work Weeks

Riva Poor's 1970 book *Four Days, Forty Hours* sparked a flurry of experiments in rearranging the 40-hour work week. Of the many versions tried, four have gained fairly widespread currency:

the 4/40 compressed work week—four 10-hour days each week. Common variations are four, nine-and-a-half-hour days and an alternating schedule of three 10-hour days and four 10-hour days.

the 3/38 compressed work week—three twelve-and-a-half-hour days each week.

the modified work week—each work day is an extra 50 minutes long, with every other Friday off.

staggered hours—five standard eight-hour days every week, but with a choice of starting times.

Let's look at each of them in turn.

4/40 COMPRESSED WORK WEEK (4/40 CWW)

In 1970, only about 40 North American firms were using the 4/40 CWW. Three years later, an estimated 3000 companies had implemented such a plan. By the late 1970s, however, the CWW was beginning to receive a mixed press. Although the CWW is still popular (between one and two million North Americans are currently working a compressed work week), there are some limits to its usefulness. One indication of the difficulties associated with the CWW is the fact that nearly 30 per cent of CWW programs are discontinued shortly after implementation, five times the comparable rate for flexitime.

For employees, a compressed work week has the advantage of making every weekend a long weekend. The CWW also reduces commuting time by reducing the number of trips and avoiding rush hour traffic.

The disadvantages are the fatigue and increased risk of accident associated with a longer working day. The long hours often pose special problems for older workers and the parents of young children.

The compressed work week is usually an across-the-board arrangement in factories or institutional settings. In most cases, all employees have to participate, including those for whom the schedule is inconvenient. However, individual office workers can sometimes negotiate a 4/40 work week, particularly if they work independently most of the time.

Initially, employers thought that the CWW would increase productivity and reduce absenteeism, but there is little evidence for this in practice. However, employers like the fact that a compressed work week reduces set-up and clean-up time. Sometimes it also provides more efficient shift coverage.

A compressed work week is often effective in providing extra coverage for peak work loads. For example, a chronic care hospital requires some around-the-clock coverage. This can be handled by three eight-hour shifts, but since the bulk of the work load comes between 8 a.m. and 6 p.m., this period could be covered by a 10-hour shift. (Employees usually work three 10-hour days one week and four 10 hour days the next, for a 35-hour average work week.)

On the negative side, employers may find that the CWW creates communication problems with customers, suppliers and parts of the organization that remain on a five-day week.

3/38 COMPRESSED WORK WEEK (3/38 CWW)

The 3/38 CWW is a bit of a misnomer because the normal schedule of three twelve-and-a-half-hour days actually totals 37.5 hours. There are two common variations on the 3/38 CWW:

- a 36-hour work week made up of three 12-hour days.
- a 42-hour work week that alternates between three 12-hour shifts and four 12-hour shifts.

The 3/38 CWW has the same advantages and disadvantages as the 4/40 CWW, with two important differences.

- it is more suitable for continuously operating facilities.
- fatigue is a more serious concern.

The 3/38 CWW is sometimes used to alleviate chronic overtime problems. Factories that operate around the clock six or seven days a week often run into problems of burnout and turnover among their employees. Replacing the three standard eight-hour shifts with four 12-hour shifts every three days means that factories can operate six days a week without overtime. On this system, factories can run for seven days a week if the average work week is 42 hours.

The 3-M Company has created an imaginative variation on the CWW in order to eliminate excessive overtime at one of its Ontario plants. The company uses three standard eight-hour shifts from Monday to Friday. On Saturday and Sunday, two shifts work 12 hours a day. The weekend employees work a total of 24 hours a week, but they are paid for 40 hours a week. They also receive a full benefit package. This arrangement has the additional advantage of giving employees a choice between eight-hour and 12-hour shifts.

MODIFIED WORK WEEKS

Modified work weeks are the "little league" version of the compressed work week. There are two common variations.

- The normal work day is extended by approximately 45 minutes. This produces one extra day off every two weeks.
- The normal work day is extended by approximately 30 minutes. This produces one extra day off every three weeks.

STAGGERED HOURS

Standard flexitime programs don't work in factories, hospitals, fire stations or other situations which require continuous staffing of line positions. In those circumstances, the best way to improve flexibility is to offer employees a choice of two or three possible starting times for each shift. For example, one-third of the day shift at a factory might start at 7 a.m., one-third at 8 a.m. and one-third at 9 a.m. Afternoon shifts would start at 3 p.m., 4 p.m. and 5 p.m. and evening shifts at 11 p.m., 12 p.m. and 1 a.m. This approach has a number of advantages.

- Employees have more flexibility and freedom of choice.
- Overlapping shifts provide an opportunity for workers to exchange information.
- Congestion is reduced in the lunch room, change room, parking lot and at security check points.

Spotlight on Compressed Work Week/Permanent Part-time

Brenda Ruttan and Sandra Green are registered nurses in the Medical Cardiology Unit of Royal Jubilee Hospital in Victoria. Both nurses are single women in their twenties, and neither has any children. Brenda and Sandra both work 12-hour shifts on a full-time compressed work week schedule. A typical rotation involves four days or nights on followed by five days off.

Brenda likes having several days off in a row because she can more easily visit out-of-town friends and family. Both nurses also spend less total time preparing for and commuting to work. On the job, the longer shift makes it easier to organize their daily tasks and complete their charting. Sandra believes that they can provide more continuity of care because they deal with the same patients for an entire day or night.

Although they may get tired if they have a particularly busy shift, both nurses say this doesn't happen often enough to be a problem. In their opinion, the extended work day has only one real disadvantage. On working days, they have a hard time fitting in such things as banking, personal appointments and shopping.

Sandra thinks the starting and finishing times of the shift are more crucial than the length of the working day. If she works from 7 a.m. to 7 p.m., for example, she has enough time for evening outings. But if the shift ends at 8 p.m., she finishes work too late to attend most events.

Nurses Jane James and Cathy Fitzgerald used to work full-time on extended shifts at the same hospital, but Jane has been working part-time since she returned from maternity leave. Cathy also switched to part-time after a car accident left her with a chronic back problem. She found working extended shifts on a full-time schedule too gruelling because she didn't have enough time off to get the rest she needed.

For Jane and Cathy, the extended shift is acceptable because they only work part-time. Even so, Jane says a 12-hour shift doesn't leave her enough time to sleep during the daytime when there are small children in the home. On the other hand, working 12 hours at a time means she works fewer shifts for the same money.

In the nursing profession, the compressed work week has been a mixed blessing. Those who have few home and family commitments regard the extended time off as an important bonus. However, other nurses, notably those with home responsibilities, are discovering that the extended shift puts a strain on their energy for other activities.

- In large factories, staggered hours diffuse rush hour traffic.

In factories, businesses and offices where the work load is lighter at the start and end of the day, staggered hours can also facilitate set-up or clean-up operations and extend hours of service.

Staggered hours have one important disadvantage: shifts must be realigned temporarily every time the plant shuts down and starts up again.

Would a Compressed or Modified Work Week Suit Your Needs?

A compressed work week will not reduce your work load. It won't solve your problem if you are burned out or overloaded. However, a compressed work week can be an attractive option if:

- you want a regular three- or four-day weekend.
- you are able to work long hours without getting tired.
- working a longer day would not interfere with the schedules of your spouse or your children.
- you can't afford to work fewer hours in order to get more free time.

A compressed work week is not recommended for older workers, for workers with health problems or for parents of preschool children. In these situations a modified work week is better because it involves only slightly longer working hours. Staggered hours may be the best option if your main problem is rush hour traffic or a family responsibility that would be helped by a change in your starting or quitting time.

A flexitime program with banked hours is more flexible than any form of compressed or modified work week. Whenever possible, flexitime is the recommended approach.

Would a Compressed or Modified Work Week Work in Your Job?

The compressed work week seems most suited to work places where:

- the work is not physically demanding or stressful.
- the danger of accidents is small.

- the work force is primarily young and few workers have parenting responsibilities.
- the normal work week is less than 40 hours.

The 4/40 compressed work week is suitable for most single shift factories and institutions. Single-shift factories and offices can both use the modified work week. In factories, the schedule usually applies to all employees. In offices, the modified work week is usually optional.

 Home Work / Telecommuting

Telecommuting is sometimes called "home work" because it means that you do all or part of your work at home.

Futurists like Alvin Toffler surround telecommuting with technology and romance; in their scenarios, everyone will one day live in "electronic cottages" connected to the office by phone, computer, FAX machine and television. These images obscure the fact that telecommuting is neither new nor necessarily high-tech. For decades, millions of North Americans have been taking work home without elevating it to a science.

One thing has changed in recent years: instead of merely taking extra work home, many people are finding it practical and beneficial to spend some or all of their regular office hours at home. Computer modems and other electronic hardware make it possible to stay in contact with the office without having to be there in person. However, the change is only a matter of degree. If you recognize that telecommuting is quite an ordinary experience, it will be easier to think about doing it yourself and to sell the idea to your employer.

There are three ways to approach telecommuting.

Partial telecommuting means working at the office part of the time and working at home when you need undisturbed privacy for tasks such as report writing, planning, budgeting and so on.

Full telecommuting means that you work from home exclusively or almost exclusively. Your home work space may contain fairly extensive telephone and computer equipment for communicating with the office.

Satellite telecommuting involves working with three or four other people in a small neighborhood office close to home. The satellite office is linked electronically to the main centre downtown. Strictly speaking, this doesn't qualify as working at home, but it offers some of the same benefits (less commuting time, for example, and the ability to have lunch with the kids).

Telecommuting sounds appealing, but it has drawbacks as well as advantages. The obvious advantages of working at home are:

- less commuting time.
- a more pleasant work environment.
- better integration of work and family life.
- the ability to work without distractions or interruptions.
- the freedom to work independently at your own pace.

Some of the disadvantages of telecommuting are:

- a sense of social isolation and alienation from co-workers.
- a feeling that you are left out of the decision-making process.
- invisibility and the possibility that you may be passed over at promotion time.
- vulnerability to abuse by your supervisor.
- vulnerability to being laid off.

The advantages and disadvantages associated with telecommuting both become stronger the more you move towards full telecommuting.

What Do Employers and Unions Think of Telecommuting?

Employers and unions both have mixed emotions about telecommuting. Employers worry about "losing control," about the difficulties of supervising and communicating with telecommuting staff, and about the extra costs associated with a work station at home. Employers sometimes worry about setting a precedent for other workers. ("If we let you do it, everyone will want it.")

On the other hand, employers are often attracted to telecommuting by the promise of happier and more productive employees. Sometimes they welcome the opportunity to reduce overcrowding in the office.

Formal, written proposals may not be the best way to raise the issue of telecommuting with employers. Partial telecommuting in particular often begins in a casual manner, without involving anyone but the employee's immediate supervisor: "I'm sure I could get the quarterly report done on time if I could stay at home tomorrow and work without interruptions." Full telecommuters often begin by working at home on a short-term, casual basis. Mini-trials like this give both you and your employer a better idea of what would be involved if you were to work at home.

Unions are under some pressure from members to expand telecommuting opportunities, but they have some serious and valid concerns.

Unions worry that at-home workers will be hard to organize, that they will be vulnerable to pressure from their employers, that telecommuting will degenerate into a piecework cottage industry like the garment trade, and that employers will try to "spy" on employees by monitoring their work through the computer.

One way to deal with your union is to avoid theoretical discussions of telecommuting. These discussions tend to emphasize the problems rather than the benefits. Focus instead on the specifics of your job and your needs.

Would Telecommuting Suit Your Needs?

Telecommuting may be the best option for you if:

- you spend a lot of time commuting.
- you have a physical disability that impedes your access to the office.
- you are recovering from a serious accident or illness.
- you work in a distracting environment at tasks that require a high level of concentration.
- you want to have some contact with your children during the work day.

Telecommuting can often give you more control over your work life. You can dress casually and do your errands in the time you used to spend commuting. You can have lunch with your children and put dinner in the oven at three o'clock. Having a sick child at home doesn't mean losing a day of work. You have the freedom to smoke, or to work in a smoke-free environment. You can arrange the lighting, the furniture, the sounds and colours of your work space to suit your preferences. You can work outside of regular office hours if you want to. You're free to take a short break to work in the garden, walk the dog, listen to the stereo, lie in the sun or take a short nap. You'll probably spend less money on transportation, eating out and work clothes.

Telecommuting may look like the ideal way to combine a job with child care, but there are definite limits. In general, it doesn't work for people with preschoolers to care for. They end up feeling frazzled, and they can't give enough attention to their work or their children. People have mixed experiences combining home work with the care of school-age children or infants. Some people rave about it, and others rage against it.

Home Work and Self-Employment

Freelancing and contract work are forms of self-employment. They fall outside the definition of telecommuting because they involve profound changes in the employee-employer relationship. However, they represent viable options for people who want to work at home.

Freelance work involves selling a product (such as a magazine article or a graphic design) rather than selling your time. The buyer and seller have no responsibilities to one another beyond the terms of the specific project in question. Freelancers are free to sell their services elsewhere and the client is free to buy from other suppliers. Freelancing has a high level of freedom and little or no job security.

Contract work involves selling your time to an employer for a fixed duration. Contract employees often get a higher hourly wage than regular staff, but they have no job security beyond the end of the current contract.

Freelancers and contract workers usually have more latitude than regular staff about when and where they work, but they have less protection because the provisions of the labour code do not apply to self-employment. Self-employed workers are on their own in dealing with abuses by their clients.

Self-employment is often suitable for professional, technical and service jobs such as woodworking, hairdressing, psychological counselling, massage therapy, small appliance repairs, engineering consultancy and furniture refinishing. However, self-employment can be extremely insecure, and no one should change from a staff position to freelance or contract status without carefully assessing the risks involved. Consider self-employment only if working at home is important enough to justify the risk. Two useful resources are *Working at Home* by Carol Zetterberg and the *Work-at-Home Sourcebook* by Lynie Arden.

A lot seems to depend on the personalities of the parents and the children involved. Some nursing mothers have found it easier to take their baby to work than to work at home. *Of Cradles and Careers* by Kaye Lowman has good examples of this option.

If telecommuting sounds made to order for your needs, stop and consider the following questions before you become too enthusiastic.

- *Do you have enough self-discipline to keep working when no one is watching over you?*

Can you resist the temptations of the TV, the laundry, the garden or the beach?

- *Will you be able to quit working?*

If you're a workaholic, you may find it hard to leave work alone if you're not physically separated from your working environment.

- *Will you have a lot of distractions to deal with?*

Do you have overly friendly neighbors? Will your spouse, parent or children be at home when you are trying to work? How much quiet and privacy can you realistically expect?

- *Do you have an adequate work space at home?*

Is it private? Is it relatively soundproof? Is it well lit and comfortable? Can you protect important files from break-ins and playful children?

- *Will you feel lonely working at home?*

This is less of a problem if you're at home only one or two days a week. However, if companionship is one of the things you like about work, you may feel that working at home requires too much of a sacrifice.

- *Will working at home interfere with your professional ambitions?*

The more you work at home, the more you will be excluded from office politics, and this could affect your prospects for promotion. If you foresee any problems in this area, try to arrange a temporary trial period before you lock yourself into any full-scale arrangement for working at home.

Spotlight on Home Work/Telecommuting

Recently, Sid Tafler became the news editor of *Monday* Magazine, a news and events weekly in Victoria, B.C. As a freelancer and journalism instructor for the previous eight years, Sid had always worked at home. He had his own office complete with personal computer, printer, and phone modem and electronic mail box service.

Sid decided to take the job at *Monday* because he wanted to be involved in the publication of a "total product." After the relative isolation of home work, he enjoys the close working contact with the four editorial staff and another 15 in the production department.

Sid does all his editing work in the office because he needs to be accessible to the magazine's other editors and writers. However, he prefers do his actual writing at home for one day a week. He finds that he can concentrate much better without the distractions of an office. With only four terminals and five staff members, it can also be difficult to get sufficient time on deadline day.

When he works at home, Sid likes "not shaving, no tie and working in the comfort of my own space." His boss doesn't object to him working at home, but the first time he failed to show up at the office, the receptionist assumed that he was taking time off, and his paycheque was docked a day by mistake. The incident made him realize that working at home is not a choice that most employees take for granted.

For Sid, computer technology increased the feasibility and efficiency of home work. He can either send his completed work directly to the office via his telephone modem or put it on a disk and transfer it to the system the next day. As a member of the Periodical Writers' Association of Canada, he uses his home computer to "network" with other writers across the country. He can also link up to a number of computer databases for research purposes.

Because his job as editor involves supervising and training other staff, Sid has to spend much of his time in the office, but he appreciates the opportunity to do some of his work at home. Since he can write more efficiently that way, he has more time during his office hours to devote to other tasks.

Would Telecommuting Work in Your Job?

Only a few jobs are suitable for full telecommuting. It wouldn't work for most management positions, but sales representatives or staff researchers could probably handle it. However, most white collar jobs involve some tasks that you can do at home just as well as you can at the office. In fact, you can often work more efficiently and creatively at home if the job requires quiet and concentration. The following tasks are well suited to the home environment: clerical work, designing, graphics, legal work, correspondence, report writing, research, programming, forecasting, writing, sales work, planning, telephone calls, data entry and organizing.

The following questions will help you decide how much of your work you could do from home.

- *What equipment do you need to do your job?*

Is the equipment expensive and bulky? Would you need two sets of equipment for home and the office? How much of your job could you do at home without expensive equipment?

- *How much do you use hard-copy files?*

Information that is stored electronically is much easier to transfer between home and office.

- *How many face-to-face contacts do you make in your job?*

You can deal with telephone contacts and correspondence from home, but the home office is usually inconvenient or unsuitable for meetings with clients or other staff members.

- *How much time do you spend in front-line customer service?*

The more you are actively engaged in front-line service, the less likely you will be able to work from home.

- *How many decisions can you deal with by phone?*

Can someone else handle situations that come up when you're away? If you are in a supervisory role, do you have a responsible deputy who can take charge in your absence?

- *How responsible is your employer?*

Telecommuting will make it somewhat easier for your employer to take advantage of you. If you have any doubts on this score, you should build some safeguards into the design of your program.

... WELL, WHAT DID YOU EXPECT ?... YOU ONLY
WORKED PART TIME...

Step Three

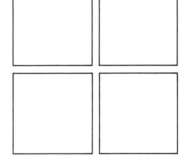

Choosing Your Time

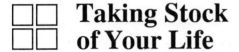

Taking Stock of Your Life

After surveying the options in Step Two, you may know exactly which option you want and how you can take full advantage of your new work schedule. In that case you may as well skip ahead to Step Four: Deciding About Money.

However, if you're still not sure which work option you like best, you may need to decide how much free time you need and what you would do with it. Step Three is designed to help you deal with these questions. Step Four will help you decide how much free time you can afford.

Sometimes work is a problem only because we haven't looked at the "big picture." We may think we want to work less, when what we really need is to reassess how much time we devote to other spheres and why. The exercise which follows is designed to help you decide what you want most out of life and what you would just as soon eliminate in order to make room for more important activities.

When you have completed the exercise, you will be able to see the extent to which your life contains the desired balance between work and activities in other areas such as family, friends, recreation, travel and so on. The exercise will also help you decide what changes you need to make in the way you use your time and whether or not a new work schedule should be part of those changes.

Instructions for Taking Stock

1. Photocopy the following nine pages. Use the copies to do your Taking Stock inventory.

2. Use a pencil to do your inventory so that you can make changes easily. Have available red and green felt pens or pencil crayons.

3. The inventory looks at eight major spheres of activity: spouse, family, social life, recreation, work/career, housework/maintenance, spirit and self. Some activities (taking the family to church, for instance) may show up in two or more spheres.

4. Go through the exercise fairly quickly at first, without taking a lot of time to stop and think about your decisions. That way your

inventory will include more of your intuitive feelings. If you really want to think about some questions, go back to them later.

5. Approach the exercise as an opportunity to explore possibilties rather than as a way of arriving at hard and fast decisions about your future.

6. Look backward in your life as well as forward. Consider not only what you think might make you happy in the future but also what has brought you pleasure, meaning and satisfaction in the past.

7. Put aside temporarily all questions of what you "should" do or "must" do. Don't be concerned about what other people think is fun. You are different. For the moment, you are interested only in *your* needs and *your* feelings.

Spouse

How close are you to your wife, husband or conjugal partner? How often is your partner the main focus of your attention? As parents, for instance, it's easy to get caught up in being "mommy" and "daddy" and to forget how to be friends and lovers. How important is your spousal relationship, as reflected in the way you spend your time together?

- Which activities with your spouse do you enjoy the most?

_____

_____

_____

- Which activities would you like to do more of with your spouse?

_____

_____

_____

- Which activities with your spouse do you enjoy the least?

_____

_____

_____

- What would you like to do less of with your spouse?

_____

_____

_____

- In an average week, how many hours do you now spend on activities with your spouse? (____)

- How many hours per week would you like to spend on activities with your spouse? (____)

Family

Family structures in Canada are becoming more diverse; therefore not all of the following questions will be appropriate for everyone. If you think of a special friend as a member of your family, if you have in effect "adopted" this friend as a parent, sibling or offspring, include that person in this sphere as well.

- Which family activities are most important to you?

_____

_____

_____

_____

- What would you like to do more of with your family?

_____

_____

_____

_____

- What family activities would you prefer to cut back?

_____

_____

_____

_____

- In an average week, how many hours do you now spend on family activities? (____)

- How many hours per week would you like to spend on family activities? (____)

Social Life

This sphere concerns all those activities that bring you into close contact with people outside your family.

- Which of your current social activities do you enjoy most?

_____

_____

- Which of your current social activities would you like to do more of?

_____

_____

- What additional social activities would you like to engage in?

_____

_____

- Which of your current social activities would you like to drop or cut back?

_____

_____

- Would you like to spend time with new friends or social groups? (specify)

_____

_____

- In an average week, how many hours do you now spend on social activities? (____)

- How many hours per week would you like to spend on social activities? (____)

Recreation

This sphere concerns all those activities that you do primarily for fun, interest or relaxation.

● What do you do now for entertainment that is most enjoyable?

_____

_____

● Which of your hobbies or sports activities bring you the greatest satisfaction?

_____

_____

● What are the most valuable or enjoyable experiences you have had in the way of travel and vacation activities?

_____

_____

● What entertainment activities, sports, hobbies or travel experiences would you like to add to your life?

_____

_____

● What entertainments, sports, hobbies or travel activities take more time than they are worth?

_____

_____

● In an average week, how many hours do you spend on entertainment, sports, hobbies and travel? Consider each week of vacation equivalent to two hours per week. (____)

● How many hours per week would you like to spend on these activities? (____)

Work and Career

- What aspects of your job(s) do you find most important or satisfying?

_____

_____

- What aspects of your job(s) do you find least important or satisfying?

_____

_____

- What work activities would you like to do more of?

_____

_____

- What courses or further training would enable you to do your job better or make your work more interesting?

_____

_____

- Are you satisfied with your current job?
  (____) yes   (____) sort of   (____) not at all

- What new kinds of work or career opportunities would engage your interest?

_____

_____

- Including commuting time, how many hours per week do you now spend at paid employment? (____)

- Including commuting time, how many hours per week would you like to spend working for pay? (____)

Housework and Maintenance

Housework and maintenance activities include such tasks as housecleaning, shopping, laundry, cooking, eating, banking and so on.

● Which of these tasks do you most enjoy?

_____

_____

_____

● Which of these tasks would you like to eliminate or spend less time on?

_____

_____

_____

● What housework and maintenance tasks would you like to spend more time on (for example, baking your own bread or redecorating your home)?

_____

_____

_____

● In an average week, how many hours do you now spend on housework and maintenance activities? (_____)

● How many hours per week would you like to spend on housework and maintenance activities? (_____)

Spirit

This sphere concerns any activities that have to do with your relationship to the larger universe. Include private spiritual practices (prayer, meditation), group practices (religious services, study groups) and volunteer commitments or "causes" that you support.

- Which of your present spiritual activities or practices are most important to you?

_____

_____

- What "causes" or volunteer activities are most important or satisfying for you?

_____

_____

- Which of your present spiritual activities or practices would you like to drop?

_____

_____

- Which of your current volunteer activities would you like to cut back or drop?

_____

_____

- What additional spiritual activities or volunteer commitments would you like to add to your life?

_____

_____

- In an average week, how many hours do you now spend on volunteer commitments and spiritual activities or practices? (___)

- How many hours per week would you like to spend on these activities? (___)

Self

Sometimes we need to relax, do nothing and pay attention to our interior lives. We need time alone to empty our minds and take care of our feelings. In this sphere, include all those activities that you do for no other reason than to please yourself.

- What do you now do to take care of yourself (the things that make you feel most relaxed and at ease)?

_____

_____

- What do you do now that helps you to feel centred and in touch with your emotions?

_____

_____

- What activities do you do by and for yourself that aren't worth the time they take?

_____

_____

- What new things would you like to do that would make you feel centred and at ease?

_____

_____

- In an average week, how many hours do you spend now on these activities? (___)

- How many hours per week would you like to spend on these activities? (___)

Inventory Summary

Hours you now spend per week	Sphere	Hours you would like to spend
	Spouse	
	Family	
	Social Life	
	Recreation	
	Work/Career	
	Housework/Maintenance	
	Spirit	
	Self	

Ranking

LIST A	LIST B
How I actually spend my time	How I would like to spend my time
1 _____	1 _____
2 _____	2 _____
3 _____	3 _____
4 _____	4 _____
5 _____	5 _____
6 _____	6 _____
7 _____	7 _____
8 _____	8 _____

Inventory Summary

After you have completed the Taking Stock exercise, take a few moments to review your responses. Have you been honest with yourself about your likes and dislikes? Are there things you might like to do (or quit doing) that you are afraid to admit? Do you consider some of your desires "too selfish?" If so, go back and revise your inventory to make it reflect your true feelings. Make sure your choices are really your own and not those which you feel would please your spouse, your children or your parents.

Take one final look at the overall picture. Are you surprised by any of your choices? Did you discover any aspects of your life that were once rich and exciting but have now become problematic? Have you lost interest in some activities that used to be important to you? Did you identify new interests or values that you weren't aware of before?

It would be wonderful if we had time to do everything, but of course that's impossible. Making choices is a necessary fact of life. "Having it all" is a glorious (and trendy) fantasy, but unfortunately it doesn't work. In order to have sufficient time to accomplish those things that are really important to us, we must be willing to let go of activities that are attractive but less important. The summary table opposite will help you decide which activities are more important to you than others.

Using your Taking Stock exercise sheets as a reference, copy the hours you now spend on each sphere into the left-hand column. In the right-hand column, enter the hours you would ideally like to spend on that sphere.

Next, make two new lists in which you rank the eight spheres in order of importance. In List A, rank the spheres according to the amount of time you spend on them now. In List B, rank the spheres according to their value and importance in your life.

Examine your two lists carefully. How do they differ? Look for spheres that rank higher on List B than on List A and mark those spheres with stars. Choose one sphere where you feel the most urgent need to expand your activities, and circle this sphere with a green felt pen.

Next, look for spheres that rank higher on List A than on List B and mark those spheres with stars. Again, choose one sphere where you feel the most urgent need to cut back your activities and circle this sphere with a red felt pen.

Now you should have a much clearer picture of the differences between the way you would prefer to spend your time and the way you actual-

...WE'RE NOT SURE WHAT SHE REPRESENTS — BUT
WE SUSPECT SHE WAS A WORKING MOTHER...

ly spend it. If there are big differences between your two lists, you may feel the urge to change everything at once. *Don't.* It doesn't work when you try to make a lot of changes too quickly. That approach is bound to fail because you will soon feel overwhelmed and give up altogether.

We recommend cutting back your activities in one sphere (the one you circled in red) and using the extra time you gain to expand your activities in another sphere (the one you circled in green). In the next two chapters we'll help you create action plans based on this approach to change.

If you implement these plans according to schedule, within six months you will have made significant changes in the way you use your time. By repeating the Taking Stock exercise at six-month intervals, you can eventually establish the overall balance you want.

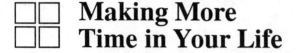

Making More Time in Your Life

In the previous section, you selected two life spheres in which you would like to make changes. You resolved to reduce the amount of time you spend in one sphere and expand your activities in another. In the next two sections, you will learn some techniques for bringing those changes about.

In order to make time in your life for new activities, you need more than good resolutions. You need a plan of action. Resolutions make us feel good and virtuous, but on their own, they change nothing. How many New Year's resolutions do you even remember in February, let alone put into practice? The following exercises in planning for change are designed to help you turn your resolutions into realities.

If you take time to complete the exercises according to the instructions, you will end up with workable plans for rearranging your priorities. However, if you merely read this section without doing the exercises, you will end up with some interesting ideas, but nothing will change.

Turning resolutions into realities is a process that requires action on three levels.

1. Recognize and confront any emotional or practical blocks to change.

2. Develop a step-by-step plan for change. Make your plan concrete, specific, realistic and actionable.

3. Start implementing your plan.

Let's take these one by one, starting with an action plan for making more time in your life. Then we'll go on to help you create an action plan for expanding your activities in another sphere.

Begin by looking more closely at the sphere you selected for pruning. Go back to the Taking Stock exercise sheet you drew up for that sphere and add any activities you may have left out. (Don't worry if it's getting messy by now. That's probably a good sign.)

Looking at the inventory sheet, ask yourself the following questions.

- *What do you get from this part of your life that has positive value?*

Dig a little when you ask this question. Otherwise, you may discover later that you've lost something you treasure.

- *Does spending so much time on this part of your life serve an indirect purpose?*

Does it allow you to avoid something scary, uncomfortable or over-whelming elsewhere in your life? Does it help you to feel less guilty about some other part of your life? Perhaps it enables you to feel self-righteous and makes someone else feel guilty.

- *Do you spend a lot of time on this part of your life by design, or by default?*

If your answer is "by default," maybe you should learn more about time management.

- *Is there a problem in this area of your life that you should be dealing with directly?*

For example, you might have lots of good reasons for wanting to work less, but if the real problem is that you hate your work (or your boss), you might do better to find a new job.

- *Are you a perfectionist who makes unrealistic demands on yourself in this part of your life?*

Maybe it's time to stop nagging yourself so much.

- *Does someone else (your boss, your spouse, your best friend) decide how much time you spend on this part of your life?*

Maybe you are letting the demands of other people "nickel-and-dime" your life away.

- *What are the practical reasons why this part of your life takes so much time?*

List all the important financial or practical constraints you can think of. Save your list for the next chapter.

By now you should have a reasonably clear picture of the emotional and practical problems you face in cutting back your activities in this particular life sphere. Perhaps you see a need to read more on these issues. A list of resources for further reading is included at the end of the book.

Now let's move on to the next step — developing a plan for change. (If work and career is the sphere you want to cut back, we'll help you develop a plan for that in Step Five. In that case, you may as well skip ahead to the next chapter, "Getting More of What You Want.")

To begin, create a Priority Profile of the life sphere in which you want to do less rather than more. Take a clean sheet of paper and draw five columns as follows:

Priority Profile

Activity	Time	Priority	Action	Time Saved

In the left-hand column, list all the specific activities in this sphere. Use the Taking Stock exercise sheet to jog your memory. In the second column, calculate how much time you spend on that activity in an average week.

When you've done this for all the activities on your list, move to the third column and give each item an "A," "B" or "C," depending on its order of priority in your life. "A"s are the most important activities for either personal or practical reasons. They are the ones you cannot drop. "B"s are desirable activities for either personal or practical reasons, but they're not essential. "C"s are the lowest priority. These activities may have some practical or personal value, but they are expendable. If you hate or strongly dislike any of the activities in your list, circle the letter in column three.

Add all the amounts of time in the second column. Does the sum match the total time you spend in this sphere of your life in an average week? If not, check to see whether you have left out any activities (those frequent "unexpected emergencies" perhaps?) or whether you need to revise any of the estimates up or down.

Now it's time to do some cutting. Look through all the activities in your list, paying particular attention to the "C"s and the ones with circles around the letters in column three.

Which activities can you eliminate altogether? (Be ruthless with "C"s and cautious with "B"s.) Write "delete" next to these in the "Action" column.Which activities can you cut back part way? Under "Action," write "reduce" next to these activities. Which activities could someone else handle as well or better than you? Write "delegate" in the "Action" column. Which activities could you do in a different way that would require less time? Under "Action," write "revise" next to these.

In the last column, next to each item marked for "Action," calculate the average amount of time you will save each week as a result of the changes you decided to make.

Total the amounts of time in the fifth column. Will you save enough time by these changes, or do you need to go back over the list again?

Write "Do List" at the top of a separate sheet of paper and rule it into four columns as follows:

Do List

Activity	Steps	Priority	Date

Now go through the first list and copy into the left-hand column all the activities you decided to delete, reduce, delegate or revise, leaving about three lines between each item.

Consider what steps you need to take to change the amount of time you spend on each of these activities. The activities you intend to delete may require no action at all. Delegating an activity will probably require some negotiation with the person or persons involved.

For every change you intend to make, ask yourself if it will produce any indirect results that you should consider or whether you should communicate with someone else about the change. For example, if you've decided to stop reading the Sunday *New York Times*, you may need to cancel your subscription. If your spouse occasionally reads the paper, too, they'll want to know of your plans to cancel it.

Next, go back over the list and assign priorities ("A," "B" or "C") to each step. Again, "A"s are urgent or very important, "B"s are of medium importance and "C"s are expendable. If any of the steps to take seem unmanageable, break them down into smaller steps.

Now that you've finished developing your plan of action, you're ready to move on to the final stage of the process—implementing your plan.

Begin setting approximate deadlines for the steps you intend to take, starting with the "A"s and working through to the "C"s. Don't try to do everything at once. Allow enough time to accomplish all the things you need to do without overloading yourself. If your overall goal is to make more time in your life, you will defeat your purpose by adding fifteen extra tasks to next week's list of chores. Don't worry if it takes six months to make all the changes comfortably.

When you've finished setting deadlines, enter the various steps you intend to take in your daily planning diary. (If you don't have a daily planning diary, go to the stationery store and buy one.)

Plan to spend half an hour in a month's time reviewing your progress. Select a date for this review and mark it on your calendar.

If you would like to cut back the time you spend in another sphere of your life, mark a date in your calendar three months or six months down the road to begin looking at possibilities in that sphere. It's easy to lose track of good ideas and good intentions if we don't find ways to jog our memories!

After all this, you've earned a break. But first, enter one more item on your calendar. Set aside a couple of hours to tackle the next section of this book, called "Getting More of What You Want." That's where you will start planning how to get more of the activities that you want and like into your life.

Getting More of
What You Want

To begin creating an action plan for getting more of what you want, go back to your Taking Stock exercise sheets. Find the sphere in which you have decided to expand your activities and add any activities you may have left out, particularly those you want to do more of. Look it over for a minute and see how it feels.

When we compare the way we would like to spend our time and what we actually do with it, we often find that practical considerations are not the main issue. If this is true in your case, some soul-searching may be in order. The following questions may help clarify your thinking in relation to the life sphere you want to enhance. If any of these questions raise particularly potent issues for you, take some time to explore them further, perhaps in your journal or in a letter to a friend.

- *Do you really want what you think you want?*

You may believe that family is the most important thing in life, even though you actually feel more comfortable and useful at work. We often vote with our feet. When there is a big disparity between what we do and what we say, we should be asking whether our heads and our hearts are really in agreement.

Take some time to sort out your real wants from your "should wants." Maybe you have made choices on the basis of what you think would be good for you instead of letting your heart speak for itself.

- *Do you refrain from doing something because you think it would be selfish or because you feel that you don't "deserve" to have what you want?*

Few people consider themselves as successful, loving, giving or accomplished as they could or should be. We are always tempted to force ourselves to be better than we are. We give ourselves rewards for doing well and withhold rewards or punish ourselves for falling short of our expectations. We treat ourselves as reluctant donkeys that need the carrot and stick in order to get anywhere in life.

The problem with this approach is that the donkey eventually gets tired of being pushed around, digs in its heels and refuses to move.

We retaliate by denying the donkey (ourselves) any more rewards. This creates a stalemate: because we aren't doing what we think we should do, we refuse to give ourselves permission to do what we want to do.

Trying to force ourselves into a particular kind of behavior by punishing ourselves never works. It only causes us to waste a lot of energy warring with ourselves. This takes all the pleasure out of life and disrupts the natural process by which we grow and become more like our ideal selves.

- *Do you let fear rule your actions?*

Fear wears many disguises. What we call boredom, laziness or procrastination may, in fact, be fear of starting something new. Even if we believe that the end result will be pleasurable, the unknown can be terrifying. And of course, fear gets stronger the longer we let it control us. If fear is keeping you from doing what you really want to do, take a look at the section on "Overcoming Fear" at the end of this chapter.

- *Are you too much of a perfectionist?*

We often put off starting a new activity because we make unreasonable demands on ourselves. If you take up running, for example, with the idea that you're going to win next year's marathon, the idea of running will seem so daunting that you may never actually begin.

- *Have you taken full control of your self-image?*

We often deny ourselves the right to do something because it doesn't fit our image of who we are or the image that others have of us. If we are male, we may think that the activity is too "feminine" or if we're female, that the activity is too "masculine." A man who considers himself liberated may decide that football is too macho, or a feminist may decide that needlepoint is too stereotypically feminine. We might consider an activity too shallow or immature. Maybe we're afraid our friends or family will tease us about it.

Whether such negative judgements originate in our own mind or from outside, they rob us of the freedom to be who we really are and to want what we really want. When we deny or disown any part of ourselves in order to protect our image, we lose the motivation to make significant changes in our lives.

- *What financial or other practical concerns prevent you from doing what you want to do?*

If time were not an issue, could you afford to do what you want to do in this sphere of your life? How much more money would you need? Would you need help with child care? Would your spouse object if you spent more time on this sphere of life?

Although practical problems often seem insurmountable, you always have a choice in dealing with them. You can see them as excuses for your inability to get what you want, or you can turn them into a "do list" of obstacles to be overcome.

Now that you have clarified your feelings about what you want, it's time for some "brass tacks" planning. Begin with a clean sheet of paper and draw four columns as follows:

Wish List

Activity	Time Needed	Priority	Time Allotted

In the left-hand column, list the activities you would like to expand. Use your Taking Stock exercise sheets to jog your memory. Next to each item, calculate the average number of hours you think the activity would require each week. If it's a one-time activity, mark it with an asterisk.

Choose the most important activities in your list, and put "A"s by them in the third column. Mark the least important activities with "C"s and the remainder with "B"s. (You will have more success if you try for equal numbers of "A"s, "B"s and "C"s.)

How many hours of free time will you gain by cutting back your present activities? (Make an estimate if you're not sure.) That's how much "new" time you will have available each week for the activities on your Wish List. Enter this number at the bottom of the right-hand column.

Now look through your "A"s and decide how much time you are willing to give to each of these activities. Enter that amount in the right-hand column. If you have time left over after the "A"s are done, go on to the "B"s and "C"s. However, if the "A"s are important to you, don't sacrifice them by trying to squeeze in the "B"s and "C"s. New activities often consume more time (and energy) than we expect, so it doesn't hurt to reserve some spare time in your week. Activities marked with an asterisk are one-shot deals. If they're important, you can probably fit them in as extras.

Take a few minutes to review the overall picture. If it doesn't feel good, play with it until it does.

Now rule a second sheet of paper into four columns as follows:

Growth Action Plan

Activity	Steps	Time Needed	Date

Look through your Wish List, pick out one activity to which you allotted time and enter it in the first column of your Growth Action Plan. Divide the activity into steps small enough to accomplish easily in a short space of time. (Don't forget to list preparatory and/or follow-up steps.) List all the steps and the estimated time needed for each one. Repeat the process for all the activities you chose from your Wish List.

Review the finished plan to make sure it's realistic. The next chapter deals with money issues, but do what you can now to resolve any other practical problems. Remember that trying to do too much too fast, even if it's "fun," will make your life more stressful, perhaps painfully so.

Next, decide when you can expect to see some concrete results from your earlier plan for making more time in your life. This is important: in order to set target dates for your Growth Action Plan, you must be able to predict when you will have more spare time available. If the answer is unclear, don't rush it. Put the problem aside for awhile and concentrate on making progress with your plan for cutting back your present activities. Leave a reminder on your calendar to review your action plan at a later date.

When you are ready to begin implementing your Growth Action Plan, look over the steps you have outlined and enter some approximate dates in the far right-hand column. Give yourself time; don't try to start everything at once.

When you've finished setting target dates, enter each step in the appropriate place in your daily planning diary. If you need the company of a friend or some other support, make those arrangements now as well.

Set a time a month ahead to spend half an hour reviewing your progress and mark the date in your calendar. Remind yourself that the process you've just completed will be useless unless you actually follow the plan outlined in your diary. As you incorporate the new activities into your daily habits, planning will become less and less important. Until that time, however, a step-by-step plan will help strengthen your resolve.

Overcoming Fear

Fears restricts all of us more than we care to admit. In *Guiding Yourself Into a Spiritual Reality*, fire-walking instructor Tolly Burkan offers the following advice for overcoming fear.

Tell the truth about the situation. If fear is controlling your decisions, acknowledge the fact. You could be telling the truth when you say, "I'm just too lazy to sign up for the course." But if you're really afraid to sign up for the course, admit it—especially to yourself.

Feel your fear. Fear is a message from inside saying, "Pay attention." Rather than viewing fear as a dictator that tells you what you can't have, think of fear as an assistant that can help you identify all the obstacles and contingencies you must deal with in order to get what you want.

Recognize your wants. When you want something badly enough, you will find a way to get it, but if you continually find reasons for not wanting something ("The course would take too much of my time" or "I'm not sure the course would meet my needs"), you undermine your power to overcome obstacles.

See yourself doing what you want to do. If you want to become a dancer, visualize a detailed image of yourself in the dance studio. Picture the clothes you are wearing and the other people present. Hear the music and feel your body moving. Imagine yourself on your way home after class. Clear, concrete images are powerful motivational tools. They block out negative thoughts and rationalizations for not doing what we need to do in order to get where we want to go.

Get support. Let someone you care about know what you want and what you fear. Recruit this person as a co-conspirator and cheering section.

Make a concrete, step-by-step plan. General or abstract goals often paralyze action because they seem unattainable. When a task seems too big to manage, it usually is. The more we divide a big job into a lot of smaller ones and focus on taking one step at a time, the less daunting the task becomes.

Decide what is the worst thing that could happen if your plan went wrong and accept it. Once we have prepared ourselves to face the worst possible consequence of our actions, fear loses a lot of its power.

Shaping Your Free Time to Fit Your Plan

Free time is only as useful as you make it. If you intend to work less in order to get involved in new projects or activities, you need to structure your free time with those activities in mind. Will you be able to use small amounts of time productively or do you need large blocks of time? Maybe you need some of each.

In structuring your time off, be realistic about your habits and your biological time clock. If you are slow to get going in the morning, don't schedule a writing project or some other creative activity for the first thing in the day. Use that time for activities you can't avoid—your regular job! Getting up and going to work will force you to make productive use of your mornings, leaving the rest of the day for better things.

Some activities are best suited to short periods (two to three hours) of regular daily practice. They include:

- time with the kids after school.
- gardening.
- strenuous physical activity or vigorous sports.
- courses that require intense concentration.
- writing (for some people).

A shorter work day is an appropriate way to make room for these activities. It has at least one disadvantage, however. It does not reduce the time you spend each week getting to and from work. This can be an important consideration if you live a long way from your work place.

A shorter work week reduces the time you spend commuting. It's also advantageous for activities that involve lengthy preparation or travel time. Making pottery or stained glass are not projects that you can easily pick up and put down, and some people can't get up the momentum for writing unless they have several free days ahead of them.

For camping or sailing trips and other excursions, it helps if you can extend the weekend by adding Friday or Monday. Recreational facilities (golf courses, health spas, campgrounds, etc.) are less crowded on weekdays, and there will be less traffic on the road to the cottage if you leave Thursday evening. Full days off can be useful for:

- freelance work.
- writing or painting (for some people).
- reading and relaxing.
- doing errands.
- day trips.
- mid-size projects.

Some activities require more extended blocks of time. If you plan to take longer trips or tackle big projects, you may need a whole week off every so often or several weeks or months at a time. If you do a lot of fishing or downhill skiing, you may want to schedule your time off "in season." Weeks or months off may be necessary for:

- travel, particularly to other countries.
- schooling.
- big projects such as building a house or starting a business.
- an extended "health break" from your job.

Large blocks of time have the advantage of enabling you to really "get away from it all." Unfortunately, unless you can make special arrangements, they also involve extended periods of time without a paycheque.

It may be possible to reduce your hours of work in more than one way: for example, a shorter work week plus extra vacation time. However, you will usually encounter less resistance from your employer if you stick to one kind of schedule change. Unless you can demonstrate the advantages to your employer of a more complex arrangement, you will be better off choosing the one kind of time off that has the most benefits for you.

Step **Four**

Deciding About Money

What Can You Afford?

In Step Three, you reviewed how you use your time now and decided how you would prefer to use it in order to get what you want out of life. Getting what you want may require working less or changing the hours you work. However, some decisions about restructuring your work time will depend in part on your financial position.

In Step Four, we will look more closely at the relationship between money and time, including the effect of reduced work time on employment benefits.

The exercises in Step Four will help you decide how much or how little you need to work to stay afloat financially. If you want to rearrange rather than reduce your work hours (flexitime, compressed work week or telecommuting), your financial picture will be unchanged: in that case, skip ahead to Step Five.

When we look at the difference between how we would like to spend our time and what we actually do with it, we usually find that money is a large part of the problem. We want to go sailing, but we spend most of our time trying to pay for the sailboat.

We need money to live, but the amount of money we need depends on the kind of lives we lead — the kind of home we live in, whether or not we own a car (or two cars), whether we vacation in a condo in Florida or in a tent at the local campground. Since most of us trade time for money (a pay cheque), the kind of lives we lead will determine how much time we spend working and how much we have leftover for ourselves.

One way to get more time for ourselves is to work less, but working less means making do with less money. If you want more time, there is no alternative: you have to cut expenses. And that means changing the way you live. A good place to start is by looking at how you spend your money now.

The first step is to go through your cheque book and calculate your average monthly expenses. Photocopy page 104 and enter current monthly expenses in the appropriate spaces. If the total is less than your current monthly income, check to make sure you haven't forgotten anything.

Study each item on your list of current expenses to see where your paycheque goes each month. Are you spending money on anything that isn't worth the time you have to work in order to pay for it? For example, how many hours do you have to work to buy lunch out every day? How much money could you save by taking buses and cabs instead of owning a car? Could you live without cablevision or weekly movies?

Take some time to brainstorm (perhaps with your spouse or a friend) all the ways you could live on less. If you've never before tried to budget your money, you'll probably find lots of room to cut your cost of living.

Next, draw up a new budget based on your minimum expenses. Here are some tips to help make your projections as realistic as possible.

- "Miscellaneous" should account for at least 10 per cent of the total in order to cover unexpected expenses.
- Beware of "robbing Peter to pay Paul." Baking your own bread may save on food costs, but unless you love baking bread, the savings may not be worth the extra time involved.
- If you plan to take up a new activity—painting, horseback riding, or a university course—be sure to include any extra costs in your budget.
- If you plan to buy a big ticket item at some time in the future—a car, a boat, a dishwasher or a new sofa—be sure to allow for it under "savings."
- If you plan to reduce the hours you work, you will probably save money in some areas (income tax, transportation, child care), but you may spend more in others (extra costs to retain full employment benefits, the cost of your new free-time activities). Include estimates of these changes in your budget.

Monthly Budgeting

	Current Monthly Expenses	Minimum Monthly Expenses
Housing (rent or mortgage + taxes)		
Heat (average over 12 months)		
Electricity		
Telephone		
Transportation (fares or car payments + gas + average monthly maintenance)		
Food		
Furniture and appliances		
Clothing		
Medical and dental		
Entertainment		
Insurance (house + life + car)		
Vacation (averaged costs over 12 months)		
Loan and/or credit card payments		
Savings		
RRSP		
Other		
Other		
Miscellaneous		
TOTAL		

When you have completed your new budget, you will know how much you need to earn in order to meet your expenses:

minimum monthly expenses = minimum take-home pay

To find out how many hours you need to work to cover your budget, divide the amount you need to earn by your current monthly take-home pay and multiply the result by the number of hours you now work each week. The answer is the minimum number of hours you need to work.

Minimum amount you must earn from your job	Current monthly take-home pay	Current hours/week	Minimum hours/week
_____ ÷	_____ X	_____ =	_____

How does this minimum work week compare to the number of hours you want to work? If you want to work 32 hours per week and you can afford to live on 28 hours per week, your problems are over. However, if you want to work 24 hours per week but need to work 28 hours to meet your expenses, you have some more thinking to do.

You can decide to accept the fact that you will have to work more to pay for the standard of living you want, or you can look for additional ways to cut your expenses. Another alternative is to find additional sources of income.

- *Do you have an extra room that you could rent to a student?*

If you own a cottage, you might consider putting it up for rent. Do you own a sailboat that you use only part of the time? If so, why not take in a partner?

- *Can you increase your income by bartering?*

Since you will have more time at home, you might consider joining a babysitting co-op. Some communities have a Local Exchange Trading System (LETS) that makes bartering easier and more flexible.

- *Could you find work outside your regular job that would be more enjoyable or more remunerative?*

Many job sharers earn additional income from self-employment: freelance writing, private practice counselling, consulting services, handicrafts and so on.

To find out how much you need to earn from other sources, divide the number of hours you want to work by the number of hours you are working now and multiply the result by your current income. The answer is the amount you will earn by working your preferred minimum hours.

Preferred hours per week	Current hours per week	Current monthly take-home pay	Minimum monthly take-home pay

$$\underline{\hspace{3cm}} \div \underline{\hspace{3cm}} \quad X \quad \underline{\hspace{3cm}} = \underline{\hspace{3cm}}$$

Subtract your minimum monthly take-home pay from your minimum monthly expenses to find how much you need to earn from other sources.

Minimum monthly expenses   _____

Monthly take-home pay for
preferred hours   _____

Income from other sources   _____

As you go through this process of balancing income and expenses, remember that it's easy to get by on a little more money than you actually need but quite stressful to live on anything less than you need. To preserve your peace of mind, plan your budget to include a safety margin of income over expenses. That way an unexpected rent increase won't sabotage your whole program.

 What Will Happen to Your Benefits?

One of the key issues in choosing a work option is the effect on employment benefits. Some work options have no effect on benefits, but others can reduce benefits significantly. Generally speaking, your benefit package shrinks proportionately when you choose an option that involves working fewer hours (job sharing and permanent part-time, for example). Options that involve rearranging your work hours (flexitime, compressed work week, telecommuting, banked overtime) do not result in any loss of benefits.

If cuts in work time are small (25 per cent or less) as in most V-Time programs, you can often negotiate to keep full benefits unless they are automatically prorated according to your salary. Most phased retirement programs and some leave arrangements also allow you to retain full benefits.

If you work 25 to 60 per cent less, you can expect the loss in benefits to be proportionate to the number of hours lost. But if you cut your hours by 60 per cent or more, you may lose a disproportionately large share of benefits. You can usually do a certain amount of horse trading, however. You can agree to give up benefits you don't care about in return for the right to keep others that you consider important.

As you look at the effect of reduced work time on different benefits, check off the benefits that are included in your current package. Then you can see what will happen to your benefits if you significantly reduce your work hours and income. Identify those benefits you want to keep and those you can do without. When you decide on an option program, you may have to negotiate a benefit package. The negotiations may go through a process of offer and counter offer in which you agree to give up some benefits in order to get a better deal on others. If you can't reach a satisfactory agreement with your employer, you may decide to withdraw your work option proposal rather than lose valuable employment benefits.

- *Unemployment insurance (UIC)*

UIC contributions are based on a percentage of income. If you reduce your income and then get laid off, you will receive a proportionately smaller UIC payment.

- *Canada Pension Plan (CPP)*

CPP contributions are also based on a percentage of salary. Reducing your salary may reduce your Canada Pension, but not always. For example, as long as you continue to earn over $25,000 per year, reducing your income will not affect your CPP contributions.

If you are raising small children, you can be on low (or no) income for up to seven years without any loss of Canada Pension benefits. You can also exclude an additional 15 per cent of your lowest earning years from your CPP calculation (about seven years for most people). Reduced earnings during this period will not affect your Canada Pension.

Generally speaking, you may work less for up to 10 years with little or no effect on your Canada Pension. If you plan to continue working less than full-time for more than a decade, contact the Canada Pension Plan and ask for an estimate of the possible effect on your Canada Pension.

- *Worker's Compensation*

Worker's Compensation is also based on a percentage of income. If you were injured or disabled, worker's compensation payments would be based on your reduced income.

- *Vacation*

In most work option arrangements, paid vacation time reflects the number of hours you work. For example, if you were entitled to 20 days of vacation per year working full-time, you would get 12 days of vacation if you worked only three days per week. This is not as bad as it sounds: in both cases you would have four weeks off work each year.

- *Sick leave*

Sick leave is usually prorated when you work less, but the overall effect is minimal since the less you work, the less likely you'll be sick on a work day.

- *Statutory holidays*

Statutory holidays may or may not be prorated, depending on your agreement with your employer. In any case, you can often negotiate an arrangement that gives you the same paycheque every week, regardless of how statutory holidays fall.

- *Registered Retirement Savings Plan (RRSP)*

Employer contributions are usually calculated as a percentage of income. Earning less will reduce the speed at which your RRSP grows.

- *Company pension plan*

Your company pension plan will be affected by reducing your income unless you can make a special arrangement. However, some plans are affected more than others.

The effect should be minor if your plan is based on an annuity or an RRSP. For example, if you worked three days a week for five years and worked full-time for the remainder of a 40-year working life, your eventual pension would decrease only about five per cent.

Most salary-based plans are not seriously affected if you work less in the early or middle part of your working life. However, if you work less in the latter part of your working life, the effects could be severe. If you cut your work time in half in the five years before you retire, your pension could also decrease by half. For this reason, older workers should always make any proposal to work less contingent upon full pension protection. Most employers will agree to special arrangements that make such protection possible.

In some pension plans, a reduction in work time will exclude you from the plan. If you propose to reduce your hours, always request a written assessment of the effect on your pension and postpone your final acceptance until you have confirmed a satisfactory arrangement to protect your benefits.

- *Medical and dental plans*

Although your eligibility for provincial medical and dental insurance will not change, you may have to pay a larger part of the premiums out of your own pocket if you reduce your hours of work. Part-time staff sometimes retain full medical and dental coverage, and sometimes they don't.

Extended benefits medical insurance may or may not be affected by working less. If benefits are affected, you may find it necessary to pay all or part of the premiums yourself.

- *Group life and disability insurance*

These benefits usually continue when you work less than full-time, but payments in the event of death or disability would be based on your reduced salary. Policy rules sometimes exclude less-than-full-time employees.

- *Short-term illness insurance*

The effect on this benefit depends on the terms of the plan. Some plans exclude less-than-full-time workers. In most cases, however, insurance payments will be based on your reduced salary.

- *Profit sharing plan*

Profit sharing is usually based on a percentage of salary. Working fewer hours will reduce your share accordingly.

- *Other benefits*

Check with your personnel department to see how any other benefits will be affected.

The Politics of Benefits

Part-time employment occupies an interesting place in the history of labour/management relations. For years, some employers have tried to cut corners by withholding fringe benefits from part-time employees and by paying them second-class wages. In reaction, many unions have come to see part-time work as bad for workers. Their solution to the problem of part-time work has been to demand that employers pay full benefits for all unionized employees regardless of their status.

On the surface, full benefits seem to help part-time workers. However, this policy has a negative side effect: it limits work place flexibility by restricting the expansion of permanent part-time employment.

The following three-tiered wage structure is a standard feature of many unionized work places.

Full-time employees get full benefits, seniority protection and predictable schedules.

Permanent part-time staff also get full benefits, seniority protection and predictable schedules.

Casual employees have no benefits and little or no job security. They also have to deal with unpredictable schedules.

On a visible cost per hour to employers, the system looks like this:

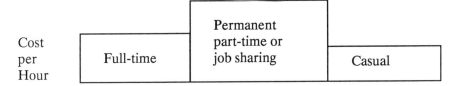

This means that employers can save money by hiring casual workers instead of permanent part-time employees. The effect on the distribution of the three classes of workers looks like this:

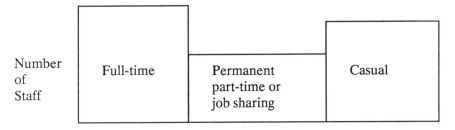

Under this system, few employees get the opportunity to work on a permanent part-time basis with full benefits, full job protection and predictable schedules. Most work full-time, which is often more than they want. If they prefer to work part-time, they often have to settle for casual employment with no benefits, no security and unpredictable schedules. The employer usually pays heavy indirect costs in absenteeism, turnover and staff burnout; no one wins.

If we were to replace this system with one in which part-time employees and job sharing staff would get benefits prorated according to the hours they work and casuals would get a prorated cash payment in lieu of benefits, the cost per hour would be the same across the board. That system would look like this:

Cost
per
Hour

Full-time	Permanent part-time or job sharing	Casual

This system would be fair to everyone because worker's composite hourly pay (wages plus benefits) would not be affected by their job status. Employers would have no economic incentive to restrict part-time employment or to over-use casuals. Distribution of the three classes of employees would be determined more by workers' needs and preferences. The result would look more like this:

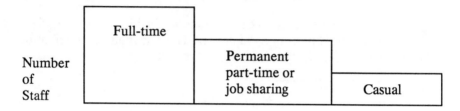

If the policy of prorating benefits extends to casual employees, it can have the positive effect of increasing flexibility by removing the economic incentive to restrict part-time employment. For this reason, most people who support flexibility in the work place also recommend prorated benefits for part-time staff.

Step Five

Designing
A
Program

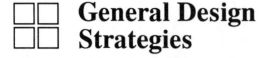 # General Design Strategies

Now that you have completed Steps One through Four, you are half-way to getting what you want. The next step is to design your new work schedule. To prepare for this step, you have:

- clarified your thinking about work.
- surveyed the nine basic work options.
- decided what you want to accomplish by changing your work schedule.
- looked at your financial needs.
- picked a work option that best suits your needs.

If you haven't decided which work option you want, go back to Step Two and choose the one that best suits your needs. (Use "Narrowing the Field" page 11 to help.) Read the section on your chosen option carefully. You'll need to know most of that information by heart when it comes time to talk to your supervisor and co-workers.

Steps Five and Six will take you step-by-step through the process of designing your new work schedule and writing a proposal to present to your employer. The design process is important because no work option is foolproof. Most work option programs are successful, but things can go wrong — for the employer or the employee or both. In Steps Five and Six, therefore, we discuss limitations — conditions under which the option doesn't work well — as well as the smart things to do in order to ensure success.

So far, you have been primarily concerned with deciding what work schedule would be best for you. But there is more to designing a successful work option program than satisfying your own needs. From here on, you will be dealing with a new problem: how to design a work schedule that meets both your needs and the needs of your employer.

The work schedule that's perfect for you may not be the kind of schedule that serves your employer's interest. This is important because you are unlikely to get what you want if your employer isn't satisfied with the arrangement. Your proposal will either be rejected in advance or cancelled when problems start to show up.

On the other hand, you shouldn't be so concerned with pleasing your employer that you fail to look after yourself. There's no point in going through the disruption of changing your work schedule if the results don't meet your basic objectives.

Fortunately, this problem rarely demands an "either-or" solution. If you use your imagination, you can design an arrangement in which both you and your employer come out winners.

The guidelines for designing various work option programs are based on general principles, but your situation may be special. Most people have some needs and wants that are unique to them. Every industry or profession has its own quirks and oddities. In real life, work option programs don't always fit neatly into one of the nine established categories.

You may find that you need to custom-design a schedule that will fit you and your job, using general principles as a starting point or an outline. In the same way that it's easier to sew fabric if you respect the weave of the cloth or chop wood if you pay attention to the grain and the knots, it will be easier to create a schedule that works for you if you respect the nature and structure of your particular set of duties.

One of the first questions you must deal with is whether to go it alone or work on designing a program that would be open to others. There is no easy answer to this question. Sometimes, it's easier for an employer to say "no" to one person than to an organized group of workers. In other situations, an employer may find it easier to make an exception for one person than to accept a proposal that would affect several staff. However, a group program sometimes creates a bigger benefit for the employer than an individual program. In that case, a group program would be more likely to attract the employer's interest.

The best solution is to design your own schedule first, making it fit your particular objectives. If it turns out that others are interested in making a similar change in their hours of work, you may decide that you would all have more strength if you act as a group. In that case, you could go on to design a collective program that will also give you the schedule you want.

Some programs (V-Time, flexitime and banked overtime) are almost always set up to provide options for several employees. However, thinking about how the program would work for your own job is a good way to prepare for the implementation of a group option.

In Step Six, Getting What You Want, we'll consider this question of group proposals and individual proposals in more detail.

As you go through the questions in Step Five, make careful notes on your responses. These notes will be the raw material for your written proposal to your employer.

When you think you have resolved all the issues and you've settled on a basic design, spend some time troubleshooting. Imagine all the things that could possibly go wrong with the new arrangement. What special circumstances might come up from time to time in your job, and how would you handle them? What kind of communication problems might result from the new arrangement? Will your new schedule cause problems for other people?

Describe your plan to a sympathetic co-worker and ask that person to play devil's advocate by trying to find the weaknesses in your design. At work, spend a week or so imagining how you would do your job with the new schedule in place. Can you see any problems?

When it comes time to present your ideas to your employer, you will have to respond to a lot of "what if?" questions. Try to anticipate possible objections. You should be ready with suggestions for coping with the problem or else have a good argument to show why the problem won't come up.

The following questions are typical of the basic concerns you are likely to encounter. Make sure you can answer them successfully.

- *Who will be involved?*

This one is easy if you are the only person affected. But if you are designing a work option program for a group of employees, you'll need to know who will be eligible and who will approve requests to participate.

- *What is the new schedule?*

For collective programs, the question is often "What range of schedules is allowable?" You will also have to know how the new schedule will affect attendance at staff meetings and staff training sessions. How will it affect statutory holidays and the scheduling of vacations?

- *Who will look after your responsibilities when you're not on the job?*

Will someone else be hired to fill in when you are away? Will an existing staff member cover for you?

- *How will you handle communication with your clients and co-workers?*

Do office procedures need to be changed? How will information be transferred? How will others keep track of your schedule?

- *How will the new arrangement affect your seniority and your employment benefits, particularly your pension?*

How can you get the benefits you want, and yet keep costs reasonable?

- *How will your employer benefit from the change?*

Will the change provide better peak coverage or extended hours of service? Will back-up staff be available to cover in case of an emergency? Will the change bring new skills or ideas into the organization? How can costs of the program be minimized?

- *How will the change in schedule be implemented?*

Will there be a trial period? If the program is open to all employees, would a needs survey be helpful? Who will be responsible for implementing and monitoring the program? What happens if it doesn't work? Are there any legal considerations to deal with? How will hours of work be recorded?

Keep these questions in mind as you go through the process of designing your new work schedule. The sections on specific work options will deal with these issues in more detail.

Before you turn to the section on your chosen option, remember this advice. First, keep it simple. Your new schedule will cause less confusion for you, your supervisor and your co-workers if the mechanics are simple and straightforward. The second rule is to use established systems whenever possible. If your work place already has a committee that deals with working hours, use that to implement the work option rather than setting up a new flexitime or V-Time committee. Don't invent a new system for recording hours if existing timesheets will work with minor modifications.

Study Your Job Before You Start

Before you can make any change to the hours you work, you need to understand the structure and the demands of your job as it is now. The first step, then, is to analyze your job in terms of the tasks involved and the way your work time is organized. For now, concentrate on identifying areas that may give you trouble and aspects of your job that will make the task of

...GREAT IDEA, FRED... I KNEW THERE HAD TO BE SOME WAY TO COMBINE WORK AND PARENTING...

designing a work option program easier. Don't worry about solving the problems at this point. That comes later, when you write your proposal.

Once you've answered the following questions, turn to the section on designing your chosen option. Make notes as you read it through. These notes will be useful when you move on to Step Six: Getting What You Want.

- *What are the subtasks that make up your job?*

We tend to think of a job as one seamless, monolithic activity. In reality, however, most jobs are a matrix of different but related tasks or responsibilities. With this in mind, try to see the parts of your job that make up the whole.

It helps to think about the ways you divide your work in order to make it manageable. If you were writing a book, for example, you would write one chapter or subsection at a time. Writing each chapter would also involve a number of smaller tasks: doing the research, making an outline, writing a first draft, editing and writing a second draft. When you have dissected your job into its component parts, mentally put them into some kind of matrix that illustrates their relationship to one another. Maybe they are not related. Some jobs consist of three or four unrelated tasks that have been linked together to fill a 40-hour week.

Now try to identify one or more tasks that someone else could do. Does this task in turn consist of a set of smaller tasks? Could someone else do any of these?

- *How many of your tasks are time-dependent?*

External factors govern the timing of tasks such as answering the telephone, giving a patient her 9 p.m. pill, attending regularly scheduled meetings or turning a screw on the next widget as the assembly line delivers it to your station. Other tasks are "time-independent." You choose the time for writing reports, answering letters, scheduling appointments, cleaning up, etc. Most jobs are a mixture of time-dependent and time-independent tasks.

Decide how much the timing of what you do at work depends on what other people are doing and how much you can control yourself. This information will be important in redesigning your job.

- *What are the natural breaks in your job?*

For teachers, work falls neatly into terms and classroom periods. Accountants can separate their work into monthly, quarterly and annual statement periods. Every hour in the day constitutes a separate work period for marriage counsellors and massage therapists. Assembly line workers and nurses divide their work into shifts.

Are there natural breaks within your work day? Can you complete a given task or set of tasks by the end of a shift or the end of a week? Can you identify certain times of the year as natural starting and finishing points? Are there slow times during the day, week or year when it would be relatively easy to work less?

You may be able to use the process of attrition to reduce your work load. If you work as a family therapist or a graphic designer, it would be difficult to reduce the number of hours you spend with a client. However, you could easily reduce your work load by taking on fewer new clients.

• *How do you handle information in your job?*

How many people do you trade information with each day? How much of the information you deal with is written down? How much information do you carry in your head from day to day? If someone were to start doing your job tomorrow, what would you need to write down that you now keep in your head?

• *Who would be affected by a change in your work hours?*

Make a list of the people who would be affected by your absence from work — supervisors, co-workers, subordinates and clients. Would your boss be able to find things in the file if you weren't there? Would your co-workers have to take extra phone calls? Without you around, would your subordinates get adequate supervision? Would they lack enough things to do? In what ways would your clients be seriously inconvenienced? Begin thinking of ways to minimize the disruption that others will experience if you work less.

• *How easy would it be to replace you?*

We like to think of ourselves as indispensable, and we don't mind at all when the boss says the firm couldn't get along without us. In fact, however, few people are really irreplaceable. Chances are that if you weren't around, your boss would find some other way to get your work done. For example, do you have any co-workers who are trained to do all or part of your job? Who does your work when you are on vacation? Who would do your work if you had a serious car accident tomorrow and had to spend six weeks in hospital?

You may need to look outside your work place for a suitable part-time replacement. Is there anyone in your circle of acquaintances who is currently unemployed or underemployed who could handle your work? Former employees who have retired or been laid off are all good prospects.

Job Sharing

Designing a job sharing program involves coming up with workable answers to the following questions.

1. How will you divide the work?

Make a list of all the tasks involved in your job. Which ones will you need to share with your partner, and which ones can be assigned to one person? Duties that require prompt action should be shared unless the partners work half-days or alternating days. How many tasks carry over from day to day and week to week? Would it be easy to divide your job into separate sets of tasks? Sometimes it works better to split a job rather than share it if the job involves little carry over or distinct task areas. When it makes more sense to divide the duties of a job, both partners should have enough "time independent" tasks to keep busy during slack periods in the work flow from outside.

You can decide to split your job 50/50, 60/40, 75/25 or in any other proportion. However, a 50/50 split is best if you are sharing duties rather than dividing them, particularly if your job involves broad areas of responsibility or the supervision of other employees. When people share the same duties, they get on better if both partners have equal responsibility.

2. How will you share time with your partner?

There are many ways to share time: for example, mornings/afternoons, one-week-on/one-week-off, half-weeks, alternate months or six-months-on/six-months-off. The following charts show how A and B can divide the work week equally by working two days one week and three the next.

Split-Week Rotation

	Mon.	Tues.	Wed.	Thur.	Fri.
Week 1	A	A	B	B	B
Week 2	A	A	A	B	B

Full-Week Rotation

	Mon.	Tues.	Wed.	Thur.	Fri.
Week 1	B	B	B	A	A
Week 2	A	A	A	B	B

In designing a time schedule, you should consider the practical demands of the job as well as your needs and those of your partner. In some jobs, partners must take small blocks of time off (half-days or alternate days) in order to minimize disruption. In other jobs, life is simpler if the partners work alternate weeks or months.

Road test your preferred schedule while you are still working full-time. Imagine that you are doing your partner's work; at the appropriate time, switch over and imagine doing your own share of the work. What information would you need to transfer at changeover time? What aspects of the job would be disrupted by the changeover (meetings or consultations, for example)? Would a different schedule be better? Should your schedules overlap so that you can plan common strategies or exchange information? Try to find the problems before they find you.

3. How will you communicate with your partner?

How will you pass on important information from customers, clients, supervisors and staff meetings? Are some kinds of information harder to keep track of than others?

Try to identify all the possible ways that something could go wrong. Next, design effective communication systems and office procedures to avoid these problems. You may want to have coffee with your partner once a week or use a changeover file, a bulletin board or a tape recorder on your desk as a way of keeping track of information.

If you post your schedule by your desk and file it with your supervisor, others will know when you are available. If you check with important contacts before you go away, you will minimize the number of times people "miss" you. The following policy will simplify matters for your supervisor and co-workers: "Always communicate with the partner on duty. The partners will be responsible for keeping each other informed."

You will need to decide whether or not your partner can telephone you at home and under what circumstances. If you don't want your work to intrude on your private life, make sure your partner knows it. On the other hand, you may be the kind of person who likes to be consulted when anything important comes up. If that's the case, make sure your partner is aware of it.

4. How will you share employment benefits?

As a general rule, people who share a job must also find a way to share one set of employment benefits. Statutory benefits (UIC, CPP, Worker's Compensation) are no problem. They will all be prorated automatically. Compensatory benefits can also be prorated: each partner can take half of the allowable sick leave, half of the paid vacation time, half of the statutory holidays.

You will have to make some decisions about supplementary benefits such as the medical plan, the dental plan and the pension plan. If one partner is covered by a spouse's medical and dental plan, the other partner can keep both benefits. Sometimes partners trade benefits: "You take the medical plan; I'll take the dental plan." Sometimes both partners pay half of the medical and dental plan premiums. With pensions, the most common solution is to prorate the accumulated years of service: for purposes of the pension plan, every year of half-time is equivalent to six months of full-time.

5. How will you control costs to your employer?

Having another person on the payroll costs an employer approximately $100 more per year in extra paper work. Most employers will accept this expense, but every job sharing proposal should try to avoid other additional costs, if possible.

To avoid extra benefit costs, partners can agree to share the same package of benefits. If partners work alternate schedules (one works when the other doesn't), they can share the same work space and equipment. Training costs will be minimal if partners are recruited from former employees.

6. How will your job sharing proposal benefit your employer?

The long-term benefits of job sharing include better morale, higher productivity, lower turnover and lower absenteeism. However, these advantages are hard to measure. If you promise higher productivity, most employers will take the attitude: "I'll believe it when I see it."

Can you design your proposal in a way that offers your employer definite, concrete advantages? For example, two secretaries could split the work day so that one partner is always available during lunch hour. In one case, an employer advertised a full-time warehouse position, but he also needed an extra person on Mondays. Two job sharers applied and offered to work three days each every week. They got the job and the employer got the peak coverage he needed.

Your job sharing proposal can help your employer avoid the need to hire relief staff if you and your partner agree to cover for each other when one is ill. Some partners also promise to work full-time while the other is on vacation or to work extra hours during peak periods or emergencies. Job sharers often welcome the extra income from such an arrangement, but some don't want to work extra hours. If that's the case, make sure your employer understands your position.

Does your partner have skills, contacts or resources that would be advantageous to your employer? If so, you should emphasize that fact in your proposal.

7. How will you find a partner?

It is possible to leave the job of finding a partner up to your employer, but there are good reasons why you should do your own recruiting. First, if you don't do it yourself, your boss may hire someone you don't like. Second, if you find your own partner, it reduces the amount of work your boss needs to do in order to say "yes" to your proposal. Finally, it usually works best if both partners participate in designing a job sharing arrangement.

By working on a proposal in co-operation with your potential partner, you will have an opportunity to test how well you get along together. In addition, working together on a proposal will help establish a more equal partnership. Your partner can also support you in getting approval to job share.

In the beginning, however, it's important to identify your own basic needs so that you can select a partner whose needs are complementary. If there's one part of your job that you dislike, for example, look for a partner who enjoys the part you hate. If you prefer to work mornings, find a partner who wants to work afternoons. Before seeking a partner, it may also be necessary to check with your union about seniority rules that could affect your freedom of choice.

Here are some questions to consider.

- *Will you and your partner share the same duties, or will you each have different tasks?*

If you intend to share the same duties, you'll want a partner whose qualifications are roughly equal to yours. You may also decide to look for someone who is strong in areas where you are weak.

- *If you intend to split the duties of the job, what tasks will you give up?*

If your partner is to have sole responsibility for some tasks, he or she had better be fully qualified in those areas.

- *What work schedule do you want? What do you consider essential, and what are you prepared to negotiate?*

- *Are you willing or able to cover for your partner in case of illness? Should your partner be willing or able to cover for you?*

- *Do you want a partner who would be willing to trade blocks of time in order to get a longer vacation?*

- *Do you want a partner with whom you can trade child care or share space at a day care centre?*

You may already have someone in mind who would make a suitable partner to share your job. If not, you will have to find ways to locate such a person. Here are some ideas to consider.

CO-WORKERS

Very often, the best job sharing partner will be someone who already knows something about the work you do. That could be a co-worker, a former employee or a person who fills in on a casual or relief basis. Women who have left work to have children are excellent potential candidates for flexible or part-time employment.

UNIONS OR PROFESSIONAL ASSOCIATIONS

Let your union or professional association know that you are looking for a job sharing partner. Some employee organizations have job placement services, and most have newsletters where you may be able to advertise the position.

WORK OPTION RESOURCE CENTRES

The growing interest in work options has led to the creation of agencies that specialize in work option information. These agencies usually maintain lists of potential job sharers. Your local Canada Employment Centre can tell you whether or not there is a resource centre in your community.

WANT-ADS

Advertising in the classified section of the local newspaper usually produces good results, although it will involve some expense and time spent in screening the replies. Consider the following example as a possible model for an advertisement.

Writer/Researcher

Exciting opportunity for experienced writer/researcher to work less than full-time. I am seeking a partner to *share* my position at a well-established firm producing periodicals for national distribution. The successful applicant will co-ordinate research, writing and editing of materials on innovative human potential subjects. Some travel required. Send resume to Box ABC.

Once you have located some applicants, you will have to select the most suitable candidates and arrange to interview them. An interviewing guide can make this process more effective. By ensuring that you have asked all the applicants the same questions, the interviewing guide gives you a better basis for comparing potential partners.

Here are some issues you may wish to deal with when interviewing candidates:

- the kind of work the job entails.
- salary and benefits.
- the applicant's work habits and how they are likely to mesh with yours. Consider particularly the applicant's apparent flexibility, ability to co-operate, organizational skills, need for recognition, and communication skills.
- the applicant's work history.
- the applicant's educational background.
- the applicant's career goals.

- the applicant's reasons for wanting to work less than full-time.
- the applicant's long-term employment goals. What would this person like to be doing in three years' time?
- your own emotional response to the applicant. Do you feel comfortable talking with this person?

Compatibility is just as important as professional qualifications. Although one candidate might have exceptional skills and experience, another less well-qualified candidate might be easier for you to work with. Factors such as personality, work habits and ability to communicate are crucial to the effectiveness of any job sharing partnership.

When it comes to choosing between likely candidates, make sure you weigh all the factors related to your own needs. In the end, you should base your decision on how well the applicant fits your personal profile of the perfect partner.

8. How do you plan to implement your job sharing arrangement?

In order to implement a job sharing plan, you will need to make some decisions about technical questions.

- *When will the arrangement start?*

- *Will there be a trial period, and if so, how long?*

- *What happens if one of the partners leaves? Will the remaining partner work full-time until a replacement is found? Who will be responsible for finding a replacement?*

- *What happens if the original job holder wants to return to full-time?*

- *Will you be evaluated separately or as a team?*

Some of these issues will be resolved in negotiations with your employer, but the negotiations will go better if you know what you want ahead of time.

 # Permanent Part-Time

Designing a permanent part-time schedule involves coming up with workable answers to the following questions. An additional suggested resource is *Part-Time Professional* by Diane Rothburg and Barbara Ensor Cook.

1. What will happen to your work when you are not there?

If you plan to work fewer hours, someone will probably have to take over part of your job. There are a number of ways to arrange this.

JOB SPLITTING

There are two ways to split a job. You can either divide it into two separate jobs with two different sets of tasks or create two shifts to deal with the same set of tasks. If you make two separate jobs, they can be of equal or unequal size. When you split a job, you can often give up the tasks that you find boring, uncomfortable or mundane, or the parts for which you feel least qualified.

You can often leave the task of filling the extra position to your employer. However, if your employer seems likely to object, you should offer to locate a suitable person. In that case, ask around among former employees, employees on maternity leave, retirees, professional associates and friends who are currently unemployed. Look for someone who has a good reason for wanting part-time work and who is comfortable with a schedule that complements yours.

Try to find someone who wants part-time work on a permanent basis; otherwise, you are likely to find yourself under repeated pressure to return to full-time. If you are working part-time as a way to phase into retirement, however, look for someone who will want full-time later: for example, a student who will be graduating or a parent whose youngsters will be entering school.

JOB SHARING

If you can't divide your job neatly into two independent parts, you may need to consider a job sharing arrangement. In some organizations, it may be necessary to classify a shared position as two permanent part-time jobs. For design guidelines, consult the section on job sharing.

RELIEF STAFFING

If you plan to make a small reduction in your work hours, a member of the regular relief staff may be able to fill in while you are away. If your organization doesn't have trained relief staff on call, you may want to suggest that your employer create such a position. You could argue that relief staff would also be useful to cover for other employees on vacation or sick leave.

The best candidates for relief staff are people with flexible schedules who do not want full-time work: students, retirees, parents of young children, and artists, for example.

CROSS TRAINING

If you hold a supervisory or senior position, you may be able to train a junior worker who could perform your duties on an acting basis while you are away. This won't work, however, if you intend to ask for more than a 20 per cent reduction in your hours.

Training a junior employee to do your job has other advantages, too. It will minimize disruption if you should get sick, go on vacation or get promoted.

STREAMLINING OF DUTIES

Sometimes there is no need to bring in new staff to take over part of your job. You may be underutilized anyway; in that case, reducing your hours will improve your efficiency. Alternatively, try to find out if someone else in the organization who is underutilized. That person may be able to assume some of your duties. Sometimes you can streamline your job by identifying duties that have become redundant and eliminating them from your job description.

Be careful about streamlining your job, however. You may end up doing the same amount of work in less time. In that case, you are setting yourself up for burnout. A few hours a week can make the difference between feeling underutilized and overburdened, particularly if your work flow is uneven.

There is another danger in streamlining your job. Suppose your financial situation changes and you need more work. If your employer is saving money because you are working part-time, you probably won't be able to return to full-time work even if you want to.

2. What will you do to minimize the disruptions caused by your decision to work part-time?

Your absence is bound to have some effect on your work place. At times, you won't be available to take calls or handle problems that come up unexpectedly. You will probably miss some staff meetings. However, you can design your schedule to minimize these disruptions.

- *Choose a reasonable schedule.*

You can make life easier for your boss and your co-workers if you arrange your working hours to coincide with staff meetings, peak times or the natural breaks in your duties. Also, the less complicated your schedule is, the less likely your supervisor and co-workers will be confused about when you are in or out.

- *Define your duties carefully.*

When you split your job, make sure you and everyone else knows exactly where your job begins and ends. That means defining your duties as clearly as possible. If you decide to keep the task of public relations and give someone else the task of market research, who will be responsible for planning a marketing strategy?

- *Maintain good communications.*

When you work part-time, you can't rely on keeping information in your head. You have to put more information on paper so that other people can find it when you're not around.

To avoid losing messages, you can designate one person to take your messages when you're away. Also keep a copy of your schedule on your desk so that others will know when you are available. If you are a supervisor, let subordinates know what kinds of problems justify calling you at home. To avoid delaying business, make sure you complete tasks, return files, return all messages, and check in with superiors and subordinates before you go on your time off.

- *Cross train a substitute.*

If you are the only one who can do certain tasks, business will slow down while you are away. To avoid delays and frustration, make sure that someone else can do everything you know how to do.

- *Use resources efficiently.*

When you split a job, you need to consider where and when the other person will work. If you both work different hours, you can avoid extra expense by sharing a work station. Alternating schedules also make it easier to take messages for each other.

- *Look for countervailing advantages.*

Working part-time usually causes some minor inconvenience for others, but it may also have some built-in advantages for your employer. When two people split a job, they can cover for each other during vacations and sick leave. Having two part-time people on staff means your employer may not need to hire extra help for peak coverage or emergencies.

Leaves of Absence

Compensatory and discretionary leaves are structured quite differently. Compensatory leave is paid leave that is part of the standard benefit package available to all employees (sick leave, vacations, statutory holidays, etc.). Provisions for compensatory leave should be negotiated by your union or in the absence of a union, by a representative group of employees. (See also "Compensatory Benefit Leaves", page 234.)

Discretionary leave is available to individual employees on request and is usually dependent on the goodwill of the employer or supervisor. Discretionary leave is often unpaid leave.

Most discretionary leaves come under the categories of personal leave, education leave, sabbaticals, deferred earnings plans and extended leave. These are all one-time responses to unique circumstances. They do not set a precedent for other employees. "Personal leave" or "leave without pay" can also include extended vacations, compassionate (bereavement) leave, extended maternity leave, paternity leave, parental leave and adoption leave.

There are some exceptions to this general pattern in smaller organizations.

- Employees can sometimes take compassionate leave as part of their normal sick leave allowance.
- Employers will sometimes consider adoption leave as an equivalent to maternity leave.
- Individuals can sometimes trade salary increases for additional vacation time. For example, a four per cent raise would be equivalent to two extra weeks of paid vacation.

In some cases, a union or employee association will bargain to make a particular discretionary leave available as an employment right. For example, the United Auto Workers union in Canada has a collective agreement that includes a provision for paid educational leave. University teachers are entitled to a paid sabbatical leave every seven years. More often, however, individual employees must negotiate a discretionary leave on their own.

Before requesting a discretionary leave, you need to decide on the kind of leave you want (the appropriate framework), who will replace you, a mechanism for transferring your responsibilities, costs and conditions of the leave, and the countervailing advantages for your employer.

1. What kind of leave do you want?

Leaves generally fall into one of three classes, depending on how wages, benefits and seniority are affected:

sabbaticals – paid leave with benefits and seniority maintained.

personal leave – unpaid leave with benefits and seniority maintained.

extended leave – unpaid leave with seniority maintained but no benefits.

The general rule when asking for a leave is to request the best deal you can realistically expect to get and negotiate downward, if necessary. When requesting a leave, find out how your employer defines each category and use the same terminology.

SABBATICALS

Paid leave may also be called "social service leave," "paid educational leave" or "leave with pay." Some employers grant paid leave indirectly by redefining the role of the employee in the organization. Employees who want time off for social service work are "seconded" or placed on "special assignment." Employees who want to go back to school are sent for "advanced training" or "employee development." Employees who need rest and therapy for drug, alcohol, family or emotional problems sometimes get paid leave under the catch-all phrase of "employee training and development."

If your immediate supervisor is likely to be supportive, your best bet may be a quiet request for "redeployment" or "special assignment." If the organization you work for sees itself as having innovative personnel policies, you may do just as well or better with a formal proposal to the personnel department.

In either case, a request for paid leave must be backed up by a solid rationale. If you can't demonstrate how the leave arrangement will benefit your employer, you'll probably have to settle for leave without pay.

PERSONAL LEAVE

All personal leave is leave without pay. It may be called "leave of absence" or simply "leave." If you take a short personal leave (up to 90 days), you can probably keep your benefits without much trouble. The stronger your justification for going on leave, the longer your employer will be willing to continue your benefits. Personal leave is a catch-all category for all kinds of unpaid time off, including:

- extended vacation time/travel.
- religious holidays.
- therapy; recovery from illness, drug or alcohol rehabilitation; rest and relaxation.
- extended maternity leave.
- time off for new fathers or adoptive parents.
- schooling.
- social service activities.
- time off to attend a loved one's funeral.
- time off to care for infirm children or parents.

EXTENDED LEAVE

Extended leave has many different names: some of the common terms in use are "inactive status," "leave without pay," "on furlough," and "care and nurturing leave." Extended leaves can last from 90 days to a year or more. If you can justify extended leave as a benefit to your employer, you may be able to retain your place on the seniority list, but you probably won't be entitled to continued benefits. Usually, time-buyer plans are classified as extended leave, but sometimes an employer can be convinced to consider such time off as personal leave. See *The Time Buyer* for more details.

2. Who will replace you?

Finding an appropriate replacement depends on your answers to the following questions.

- *How long will you be gone?*

The longer the leave, the more suitable and qualified your replacement must be.

- *Do you have a choice about when to take the leave?*

Your replacement will have less difficulty handling your job if you can take your leave during a slack period.

- *Do you know when you will be returning to work?*

If you know the date of your return, your employer can offer your replacement a contract for a fixed period of time. Otherwise, you will have to find a replacement who will accept an open-ended arrangement.

- *Will you be available to consult?*

If you are taking a leave to sail around the world, you won't be available for telephone consultations. In that case, your replacement needs to be fully briefed in advance and capable of doing the job without your help.

In making your leave proposal, suggest a practical means of finding a suitable replacement. There are a number of ways to find someone who can handle your job effectively on a temporary basis.

- *Rehire a former employee.*

Is your predecessor available for temporary employment? Can you find a former employee who has retired and would like to return to work temporarily? What about an employee who quit to have children or go back to school? Who covers for you when you are on vacation?

- *Bring in a professional associate.*

Conferences, unions and workshops often bring us into contact with people who have skills similar to our own. Is there anyone among your circle of work-related acquaintances who could take over for you?

- *Have a co-worker (or co-workers) cover for you.*

Do you have an assistant or an associate doing a less demanding job who could take over while you are away? It may be easier to find a temporary replacement for that person's position than your own. The person might also welcome such a change, even if it's only temporary.

If you plan to take your leave during a period when the work load in your company is lighter than usual, a number of co-workers may be able to share your duties.

- *Advertise.*

You can leave it to the personnel department to find a replacement, but personnel may choose a replacement you don't like or use the lack of replacement staff as a reason for denying your request for leave. For a relatively small investment, you can advertise the position in the Help Wanted Section of the newspaper. (Have replies sent to a box number at the newspaper in order to preserve your privacy.)

- *Leave your work until you get back.*

Some jobs are built around projects that can be delayed for a short period of time. In other cases, work will pile up in your absence.

If you can't afford an unpaid leave and you are willing to work overtime when you get back, you may be able to get a paid leave on the understanding that you will be responsible for catching up on accumulated work. This is not a recommended strategy, but it may work out if the leave is short and not health related.

3. What mechanisms will you use to transfer your responsibilities?

There are a lot of things your replacement will need to know in order to take over for you. When you return, you will need to know about things that have changed during your absence. How will this information be exchanged?

In a profession like nursing, most jobs are relatively standardized, and short orientation programs for new staff are already in place. In these kinds of jobs, changeover usually requires little planning. In other positions — for example, the live-in houseparents of a group home for disturbed adolescents — an elaborate changeover system may be needed. This is often true for highly specialized jobs or jobs that involve large projects, strong personal relationships or quick responses to a crisis.

The longer you plan to be away, the more complex your job is and the more inexperienced your replacement is, the more attention you should give to developing a careful changeover plan. A number of mechanisms can help facilitate the changeover process.

- *Use relief staff already in place.*

It costs money for your employer to train a replacement, so it's more economical to use the person who normally covers for you when you are sick or on vacation. Perhaps your replacement could stay on as a relief when you return. In that case, your employer would get more benefit out of training your replacement.

- *Time your leave carefully.*

Most jobs have natural transition points or slack periods when it's easier to fit in a new person. For example, an accountant could time her leave to coincide with standard periods in the accounting year.

- *Allow for adequate overlap.*

The more complex and involved your job is, the more time you'll need to spend briefing your replacement and debriefing at the end of your leave.

- *Complete outstanding tasks before you go on leave.*

Arrange to finish old tasks and put new tasks on hold at the beginning and end of the changeover period. This will simplify the transfer of duties. All files should be kept up to date and in good order.

- *Create a changeover file.*

You can minimize confusion by leaving a good set of briefing notes for your partner. Reminders in the desk calendar ("March 15 timesheets due") and instructions next to infrequently used equipment can also help.

- *Cross train some co-workers.*

Before you go on leave, teach one or more of your co-workers the basic duties of your job. They can help your replacement with problems that come up while you are away.

- *Check in occasionally.*

Set aside a time each week to call in during the first couple of weeks of your absence. This will give your replacement a chance to ask questions while learning the ropes.

- *Lighten the load for your replacement.*

If your job is a particularly demanding one, arrange for a co-worker to take over one or more of your duties, at least during the initial period of your absence. This will increase the chances that your replacement will do a good job.

4. Are you prepared to negotiate?

Your leave will cost your employer some expense: the cost of training a replacement, any wages you receive while on leave and the cost of any benefits that you retain while on leave.

Designing a leave request is a difficult balancing act. You must establish conditions that will make the leave affordable for you and yet keep costs low enough so that your employer will grant the leave. Since the conditions of a discretionary leave are negotiable, you must be sure about what you want and also what you can afford to accept.

5. How can the arrangement benefit your employer?

You are unlikely to get a leave on advantageous conditions unless you can design your request in a way that offers some benefit to your employer. Sometimes there are natural advantages. For example, if a senior teacher takes a year's leave of absence and is replaced by a junior teacher, the differential in salaries will usually more than cover the cost of maintaining the senior teacher's benefit package.

If you plan to go to Europe for a year, you may be able to do a certain amount of work-related research. This might induce your employer to maintain your benefit package or pay part of your expenses. If you take time off to fulfill a social service commitment, you may be able to convince your employer to keep you on the payroll as a public relations gesture. Similarly if you are taking leave for education that is work related, you may be able to justify a request for some financial support from your employer.

V-Time

V-Time, or voluntary reduced work time, is a comprehensive personnel program available to all employees who want to participate. That means two levels of design are involved: the design of the overall system and the design of individual work schedules. To design an individual work schedule under V-Time, use the guidelines for permanent part-time if you plan to take your time off in short blocks. If you plan to take longer periods of time off, consult the guidelines for designing a leave of absence.

The design of an overall system for V-Time rests on the choice between a number of design options. Some choices will be fairly arbitrary, and some will be necessary to help the program meet specific goals.

1. How many time-off options will be available?

The fewer the options, the easier V-Time is to administer. More options increase the possibility that the system will meet everyone's needs and wants. Most programs offer between six and 12 options.

2. What time-off options will be available?

The best way to meet people's needs is to ask them what they want. A needs survey will help determine what patterns of time off appeal most to the employees in your organization. A needs survey also helps locate support for the program.

If the needs survey is the first step in the design process, the written proposal can include suggestions for specific options. If a needs survey isn't available, the proposal can suggest a sample range of options, on the understanding that the final range of options will be based on a future needs survey. A fairly standard range of options would include 2.5, 5, 10, 20, 25 and 40 per cent time off. Job sharing can be included within a V-Time framework if the available options include 50 per cent time off.

...IT FEELS GREAT... WHAT USED TO BE MY 'OFF' DAY
IS NOW MY DAY OFF...

3. What are the most convenient percentages?

If the normal work week is 40 hours, any multiple of 2.5 per cent will result in an even number of hours off per week. If the normal work week is 35 hours, steps of 2.875 per cent will result in an even number of hours off per week.

If the needs survey shows that some forms of time off are especially popular, these should be included in the range of options. If several people like the idea of a work day that is an hour shorter or a day off every other week, the options should include cuts of 12.5 per cent and 10 per cent.

4. How frequently will participants be able to sign on?

Most programs allow participants to sign on every six months or every 12 months. The shorter time frame is more flexible and responsive to individual needs, but the longer time frame is easier to administer.

5. When will participants be able to sign on?

Some programs allow entry at the beginning of every quarter, while others offer continuous entry. Continuous entry means you can sign on for a six- or 12-month cycle at any point in the year.

Specified entry dates make it easier to co-ordinate relief staffing. For example, if the personnel manager knows on March 1 that she will have 15 data entry staff working 10 per cent less from April 1 to October 1, she knows that she will need to hire one full-time and one half-time relief worker for that period.

Continuous entry is more responsive to changing conditions. If an employee's physical health or mental state changes suddenly (or if a family member suddenly develops physical or emotional problems), continuous entry allows that employee to get immediate relief from stress.

6. What changes are required in the benefit package?

Benefit packages can be prorated in different ways. These are discussed in more detail in Steps Four and Six.

Before deciding how you want to deal with benefits, check with external agencies that administer specific benefits—the group life insurance plan, the dental plan, the pension plan and so on—to see if they place any

Sample V-Time Benefit Chart (Part 1)

Time-off option	UIC, CPP, Worker's Comp.	Statutory Holidays	Sick Leave	Vacation Time	Seniority
Full-time	Full	8 hours each	100 hours/year	120 hours/year	Full
2.5%	Prorated 2.5 %	8 hours each	100 hours/year	120 hours/year	Full
5%	Prorated 5 %	8 hours each	100 hours/year	120 hours/year	Full
10 %	Prorated 10 %	7.25 hours each	90 hours/year	108 hours/year	Full
20 %	Prorated 20 %	6.50 hours each	80 hours/year	96 hours/year	Full
50 %	Prorated 50 %	4 hours each	50 hours/year	60 hours/year	Full

restrictions on hours of work. Also find out whether the payroll system is designed to handle nonstandard benefit packages and whether employee contributions or cash-in-lieu payments are possible.

When you have established an overall framework, give each participant a chart which clearly outlines the effect on benefits. The chart should be accompanied by notes that explain the changes in benefits, particularly those which affect pensions and statutory holidays. These are the two areas that are most likely to cause confusion.

The chart above shows the effect on benefits of a typical V-Time program. Notice that some benefits are not affected by cuts of less than 10 per cent, and the pensions of older employees are protected.

Participants should always have the right to return to full-time with full (calendar) seniority. This is especially important if V-Time is offered as an alternative to layoffs.

Sample V-Time Benefit Chart (Part 2)

Time-off option	Pension Plan Contribution*	Medical Plan	Dental Plan	Extended Medical
Full-time	Full	Full	Full	Full
2.5 %	Prorated 2.5 %	Full	Full	Full
5 %	Prorated 5 %	Full	Full	Full
10 %	Prorated 10 %	Full	Full	Employee pays
20 %	Prorated 20 %	Employee pays half	Full	Employee pays
50 %	Prorated 50 %	Employee pays half	Full	Employee pays

* Contributions for employees over age 55 will remain at the full-time rate.

7. Will the program be able to accommodate other work options?

If the payroll structure for V-Time is well designed, it will also be able to accommodate job sharing, permanent part-time, phased retirement and short-term leaves of absence. Such a structure can streamline personnel practices while at the same time offering substantial flexibility.

8. What happens when there are disagreements?

Sometimes a particular supervisor will refuse to allow subordinates to participate in V-Time. Sometimes a supervisor and an employee can't agree on a schedule for the employee's time off. Supervisors and employees may also disagree about the interpretation of rules governing statutory holidays, sick leave, etc. It is useful to designate an "umpire" who will arbitrate and mediate these disagreements. The umpire should be someone who knows the rules well, who is good at mediation and who won't be seen as a partisan for either labour or management.

9. How will the system keep track of time off?

It is easy to keep track of simple schedules that involve one hour off every day or one day off every week. Other schedules are more difficult: for example, if someone takes every Wednesday afternoon off, plus 10 extra days of vacation annually. The best system for tracking V-Time hours involves making a new category or column on each employee's time sheet. V-Time hours can be recorded exactly like sick leave, with a running balance of hours "earned" and "used" during each pay period.

10. Who will be eligible for the program?

In some programs, V-Time is available to all employees. In other programs, access is restricted to nonmanagerial staff or to staff who have completed a certain service requirement. In order to avoid resentment, eligibility criteria should be as broad as possible.

11. How do employees apply for participation in the program?

Most programs use a standard application form which the employee submits to the department supervisor or the personnel department. A simpler form is used for renewals unless the employee wants to change the previous schedule. Schedule changes are treated like first-time applications. Depending on the program, the application may or may not need the approval of the V-Time umpire, the personnel department or the supervisor's superior.

12. What rules will govern the rotation of relief staff?

If 10 assembly line workers each want one half-day off each week, only one relief worker may be required. But what if all 10 workers want Friday afternoon off? Will V-Time participants share relief staff on a first-come, first-served basis, on the basis of seniority or on the basis of some other system?

To avoid conflicts, the rules governing the use of relief staff should be clearly spelled out, and all participating employees and their supervisors should have a copy of these rules.

13. What rules will govern the design of individual schedules?

Employees and their supervisors are responsible for negotiating individual V-Time schedules. However, some rules should apply in order to prevent abuse and avoid unrealistic requests. The following mechanisms can help ensure that individual schedules will be workable.

- *Personnel budgeting by department*

Wages saved as a result of V-Time should remain within the branch or department to be used for relief staff, except when the program has been specifically designed to avoid layoffs associated with a lack of work.

- *Full briefing packages*

All applicants should receive a complete briefing package on V-Time to assist them in drawing up workable programs.

- *A comprehensive sign-on procedure*

The V-Time application form should include questions on a) the exact terms of the proposed schedule b) arrangements for sick leave and statutory holidays c) arrangements for attendance at staff meetings d) plans for minimizing disruption caused by the employee's absence from the work place and e) a plan for reassigning or eliminating the appropriate percentage of the employee's regular work load.

- *A review process*

All V-Time applications should be approved by the V-Time umpire. The umpire must be satisfied that neither the employee nor the employee's co-workers will be expected to do more work in less time. The umpire should also ensure that appropriate steps have been taken to avoid disruption in the flow of work. If employees and their supervisors are having difficulty reaching agreement, the V-Time umpire can be requested to help with the design process.

- *Clearly spelled-out rules*

Briefing materials should be absolutely clear about any restrictions on time-off options for particular groups of employees. Some restrictions may be justified by operational considerations. For example, a hospital may be able to accommodate a nurse's request for a full day off every week but not a request for shorter shifts. A university may consider it unworkable to have any support staff on vacation during the first month of term but be willing to approve extended vacations during the remainder of the year.

For more comprehensive technical information on V-Time, see *V-Time: A Matter of Time,* available from New Ways to Work, 149 Ninth Street, San Francisco CA 94103. $30.00 U.S. postage paid.

Banked Overtime

Banked overtime programs are usually designed for groups of employees who hold relatively interchangeable positions in factories that operate almost continuously. If you have a one-of-a-kind job, you may be excluded from the formal banked overtime program in your work place. Occasionally, however, a single individual can negotiate an informal arrangement to bank extra hours. You are more likely to be able to arrange some sort of low-key hours banking agreement if:

- you have visible health or burn-out problems.
- you are a particularly valuable or indispensable employee.
- you are a long-term employee with a good work record.
- you have a good relationship with your supervisor.

Any of these conditions will provide an opening basis for your request. If you can also devise a practical plan for covering your work during your time off, your chances of success are good.

Individual arrangements should cover the same issues as a full-scale hours banking program, but in as simple and uncomplicated a way as possible. Individual arrangements are often settled informally by agreement between the employee and the immediate supervisor. In securing such an agreement, finesse is usually more effective than trying to force the issue.

Whether the banked overtime arrangement is geared for an individual or a group, every system must solve five basic design problems.

1. How will the program deal with the need for relief staff?

Relief staffing is the core of any banked overtime program. Two things are likely to happen if relief coverage is inadequate: either you will never get to collect the free time you have banked or your co-workers will have to carry an extra load in order for you to take time off.

The most common solution is to hire full-time relief staff who can be booked on a rotation basis. The relief staff usually work Saturdays or Sundays as well, in order to reduce overtime for regular employees. Relief staff are usually trained to cover for several different positions. In most cases, the relief pool is large enough to cover for regular employees on sick leave, statutory holidays and vacations. The same pool of relief workers can also cover for employees on V-Time.

In some programs, relief staff are guaranteed a minimum number of days each week and receive a full benefit package regardless of how many hours they work. Because full-time relief staff must be well trained as well as flexible, they are usually recruited from the firm's senior employees. When overtime levels are unpredictable, some staff must be kept on temporary or auxiliary status. These persons are usually hired for entry-level line positions rather than as relief staff.

In some firms, relief staff have the option of working less than full-time. Sometimes regular employees would prefer to work two, three or four days a week because of heavy outside responsibilities (usually parenthood or schooling) or because they want more time off before retirement. A permanent part-time relief job is often more convenient for these employees than a normal line position.

The design for relief staffing should also consider recruiting people who would require a minimum of training or orientation. These include employees who have been laid off, early retirees, student summer replacements and employees who have left the job in order to start a family.

Banked overtime programs do not always require hiring special relief staff. Some businesses have predictable peaks in their work load. For example, an accounting firm that needs five tax accountants for most of the year may have enough work for eight tax accountants from January 1 to April 1. If the firm keeps six tax accountants on the payroll, all six would have to work overtime in January, February and March. However, during the rest of the year they could use their banked overtime to take long vacations on a rotating basis so that only five would be working at any one time.

This approach involves setting staff levels somewhere between peak needs and minimum needs. It has the advantage of creating a stronger sense of equality and team spirit than a system that uses special relief staff. However, this approach may require more work stations.

2. Will relief staff be available for all jobs?

Trained relief staff can move in and out of line positions (nursing, police work, most factory jobs, etc.) fairly easily. Mechanisms for covering other jobs (managers or employees who service ongoing clients, for instance) are more complicated and require careful planning.

People in these positions often have a hard getting any time off, even though they may need a break as much or more than other workers. People who are left out of a banked overtime program (particularly managers) may feel envious or resentful. For this reason, a banked over-time program is less prone to sabotage if it is available to employees at all levels of the organization.

The following strategies can be used to provide relief coverage for positions with complex duties.

- *Cross training*

A line employee can be cross-trained as an acting manager. (The line employee's regular duties can be more easily covered from the relief pool.) This approach also provides back-up for vacations and sick leave.

- *Extended vacations*

Regular vacations can often be extended without the need to hire spe-cial relief staff.

- *Soft loading*

Responsibilities can be adjusted to create periods of heavier and lighter work loads. During a slow period, the employee can take oc-casional days off.

- *Delegation*

By temporarily delegating specific tasks, an employee may be able to get far enough ahead to take some time off.

- *Relief by retirees or ex-employees*

Sometimes an employee's predecessor can be called back to work as relief staff.

3. How will relief workers and regular staff exchange information?

Without adequate mechanisms for communication, important infor-mation may be lost or delayed. Communication mechanisms include com-pleting tasks at the end of each shift, making written notes, keeping other staff informed about the status of important projects, and leaving messages and reminders. Full-time relief staff should receive all staff memos and at-tend staff meetings if possible.

4. What rules will govern the allocation of time off?

A banked overtime program needs a rational system for allocating time off. These systems are always somewhat arbitrary, and they often have unforeseen consequences. It's particularly useful to ask participants for their input on this part of the plan. Here are some questions to consider.

- *Can employees take time off before they have earned it?*

This is usually called *anticipatory time off.*

- *Is it mandatory to bank overtime or can employees request compensation in cash?*

Many programs allow a choice. However, mandatory hours banking may be necessary in order to simplify the use of relief staff. Optional cash payments would not be a feature of programs designed to avoid layoffs.

- *Is there a limit on how many hours an employee can bank?*
- *Which employees will have first choice of time off?*

In order to ensure adequate staff coverage, employees must usually sign up for time off on some kind of roster. If the company employs five full-time relief staff, for example, five relief "slots" will be available each working day. (In many programs, the time-off roster also serves as the duty assignment roster for relief staff. The same roster is often used to allocate vacation time.)

Rules governing the order of signing up are essential because the last people on the roster will have more limited choices than those who sign up first. Rules should be both fair and simple to administer. It also helps if people can book time off far enough in advance to make plans. Some organizations allocate time off by seniority, and some use a system of rotation. Some allocate time off on a first-come/first-served basis; others give priority to employees who have accumulated the most banked overtime.

An additional question concerns the length of time off. Will employees be able to take a day at a time or will they have to take consecutive days? If someone books five Fridays off, for instance, that blocks one relief slot for five weeks and limits the options for others. Some programs avoid this problem by restricting time off to one-week blocks. Others restrict the choice to single days.

5. How will your employer benefit from the program?

A banked overtime program is not cost free. Therefore, it must offer some advantages to the employer. For example, banked overtime is more expensive than regular overtime but more manageable than trying to cover extra hours with casual workers. (In order to keep a 200-person pulp mill open on Saturdays, an employer would have to hire 200 casual workers, but a banked overtime program could do the same job with 30 or 40 full-time relief staff.)

Banked overtime often improves morale and reduces absenteeism, accidents and staff turnover. It may also improve efficiency if the same relief staff can be used for vacation and sick leave coverage.

Relief workers should always be members of the union and get the same wages and benefits as regular employees. Similarly, the value of banked overtime should always be equivalent to standard overtime rates. Otherwise, the employer may use overtime excessively—which defeats the original purpose.

Salaried employees are an exception to this rule because they rarely receive any compensation for overtime. In that case, straight-time compensation is an improvement over nothing at all.

Phased Retirement

The first step in designing a program is to choose the type of phased retirement you want.

- If you can't afford a cut in income, you'll need a **company-paid program**. Company-paid programs offer only short-term reductions in work time (six to 12 months).

- If you want maximum flexibility and the option of reducing your work time over a long period (up to 20 years), you will have to accept an **employee-paid program**. Employee-paid programs involve a significant loss of income.

- If you want to reduce your work time gradually over a period of one to five years and you can only afford a small cut in income, a **partial pension scheme** is the best option.

- If the work schedule you want is available through another arrangement (V-Time, permanent part-time, leave of absence or job sharing), you can choose the **integrated option** approach.

- If you want the opportunity to do temporary or part-time work after you retire, a **post-retirement work pool** will be your best option.

COMPANY-PAID PROGRAMS

Company-paid programs usually result from a negotiated union demand or a request from a group of employees. They are rarely established in response to an individual proposal. (Employers are reluctant to create a precedent for other employees.) If you are determined to have a company-paid program, you will need strong support from your union or your co-workers.

Company-paid programs are characterized by the following conditions.

- The benefits are short-term — usually six months to a year.
- Cuts in work time are relatively small — rarely more than 10 or 20 per cent.

- Time off can take the form of a shorter work week or extended vacations (often the latter).
- Employees receive full salary.
- Pensions and benefit packages are unchanged.
- The option is open to all employees who have reached the required age and/or years of service.
- All participants can attend pre-retirement planning courses on company time.
- Most programs include provisions for training the retiring employee's successor during the phasing-out period.
- All eligible employees and their supervisors receive information packages outlining the terms of the program.

Employers can be encouraged to establish company-paid programs as a gesture of good will to retiring employees, as a reward for loyalty to the organization or as a way to expedite successor training. Because they are costly to employers, company-paid programs usually require some hard bargaining by unions.

EMPLOYEE-PAID PROGRAMS

An employee-paid program can be a job benefit negotiated by the union or a group of employees. In that case, the structure would be the same as a partial pension scheme but without the pension. The other option is an employee-paid program designed for a single individual. This is essentially the same as a permanent part-time arrangement, except that the employee and the employer both continue contributing to the pension plan as though the employee were working full-time. The pension plan would also need to be adjusted in order to permit payments based on contributions rather than salary.

Companies often resist changes to the pension plan, but you can argue that a system of pension payments based on contributions is likely to become increasingly necessary as more and more employees start working non-standard hours.

For employers, employee-paid programs are relatively inexpensive and easy to administer.

PARTIAL PENSION SCHEMES

Partial pension schemes are also a benefit provided by the employer in response to a union demand or a proposal by a group of employees. Because partial pension programs are relatively inexpensive for the employer, they are easier to negotiate than company-paid programs.

Partial pension schemes are usually characterized by the following conditions.

- The option is open to any employee within five years of retirement age.
- Options usually include a four-day week, a three-day week or half-time.
- Benefit packages are usually unchanged.
- The employer and the employee both contribute to the pension plan as though the employee were working full-time. The terms of the pension plan are adjusted to base pension payouts on contributions rather than salary.
- Employees are paid according to the hours they work, and this income is supplemented by a partial pension. The partial pension is usually calculated by multiplying the percentage of free time by the percentage of full-time pay expected at retirement. (A person working 40 per cent less and eligible for a 70 per cent pension on retirement would receive a partial pension equal to 28 per cent of normal earnings in addition to 60 per cent of salary. Net income would be 88 per cent of full-time salary.)
- The partial pension is sometimes paid out of pension fund surpluses, sometimes through a separate pension fund and sometimes out of the employee's individual pension account. Since this latter approach will reduce the employee's ultimate pension by five to 15 per cent, participants should be clearly informed of the terms of the scheme.
- Partial pension programs usually include pre-retirement planning courses, successor training programs and information packages for participants.

INTEGRATED OPTION PLANS

If your firm already has a job sharing, leave, permanent part-time or V-Time program, you can try to work out a phased retirement arrangement by requesting a change in the pension plan. You can do this individually or through your union.

Individuals on reduced work schedules should have the option of contributing to the pension plan as though they were working full-time. Pension payments should be based on contributions to the plan rather than on earnings. Under this arrangement, an individual could work part-time for any number of years and still collect a full pension.

POST-RETIREMENT WORK POOLS

Many Canadian companies offer part-time or temporary jobs to retired employees. To initiate such an arrangement, write a letter to the personnel department outlining your qualifications and areas of expertise and the kind of work you want (part-time, temporary, special projects, etc.).

Unions and employee associations can also be effective in persuading employers to establish post-retirement work pools. These programs require little administration—often nothing more than an information package and an application form for participants. Intelligent employers can usually see the advantages of having an experienced and stable pool of back-up staff.

In its effect on the work place, phased retirement raises the same issues as other part-time work schedules. Once you have selected the type of phased retirement you want, use the design guidelines in "Permanent Part-Time" on page 130 to work out the details of your program.

Flexitime

Flexitime is most often established as a program for an entire work place or for specific classes of employees. For this reason, our design discussion will focus on group programs.

In rare cases, a highly valued or long-standing employee or someone who works independently of other staff will be able to negotiate an individual flexitime schedule. Although the mechanics of such an arrangement are usually simpler than the mechanics of a group program, the design questions remain the same.

1. What rules will govern participation in the program?

Sometimes it is possible to divide a work force into three groups: "automatically eligible," "eligible with permission" and "ineligible." The first group would include only those job classifications that are clearly amenable to flexing. The second group would include jobs where flexing might create problems, and the third group would include jobs where flexitime would be clearly unworkable.

Many programs place management personnel in the "ineligible" category. This can cause unnecessary resentment and may undermine support for the program.

2. How will employees apply to participate and who will rule on eligibility?

In most arrangements, employees who are "automatically eligible" do not have to apply; they can begin flexing as soon as the program is operational. Employees in the "eligible with permission" category usually apply to an hours of work committee made up of both labour and management representatives. This committee and the applicant then look at the duties of the position and decide on a suitable schedule. Most committees have a set of guidelines that must be satisfied.

- The schedule must meet the needs of the job.
- Any necessary relief coverage must be arranged.
- The work of the unit or department must not suffer.
- The program must be approved by the employee's supervisor and/or unit manager.

Sometimes the hours of work committee has authority to make special arrangements for specific individuals: for instance, to offer flexitime without the normal hours banking privileges or within a smaller bandwidth. This is often a useful provision because it gives the committee more flexibility than if they were restricted to a simple "yes" or "no."

3. What bandwidth will apply?

Bandwidth refers to the morning and evening limits on working hours. Common bandwidth choices are 7 a.m. to 6 p.m. and 7:30 a.m. to 5:30 p.m.

Determining an appropriate bandwidth often involves striking a balance between conflicting gains and losses. The gains of a longer bandwidth are:

- longer hours of service to the public.
- less pressure on scarce equipment.
- better accommodation to the needs and preferences of employees.
- less office crowding and more efficient working conditions.
- reduced long distance telephone costs.

The losses associated with a longer bandwidth are:

- more hours to cover (particularly for support services like switchboards).
- more difficulty co-ordinating activities within staff teams (more chance that the person you need to talk to won't be there).
- slightly higher hydroelectric and heating costs.
- more difficult to supervise.

4. What core hours will apply?

Core time ensures that the organization is working at full strength when the work load is heaviest and that schedules overlap sufficiently to allow for meetings and intra-staff communication. Popular core time choices are 10 a.m. to 2 p.m. and 10:30 a.m. to 3 p.m. The most flexible flexitime programs do not have a core time at all, but this approach is effective only when the work involved is both self-directed and independent of clients and other staff.

Like bandwidth, the choice of core hours is often a trade-off between gains and losses. The gains associated with a longer core time are:

- greater ease of communication between staff.
- a longer period of peak coverage.

The losses associated with a longer core time are:

- less accommodation to the needs and preferences of employees.
- greater limitation on the available bandwidth.

5. Will flexibility be permitted at mid-day?

A common mid-day flex is noon to 2 p.m., but many programs omit the mid-day flex as an unnecessary complication. Lunch hours add to difficulty of staff coverage at mid-day and the problems associated with a mid-day flex. Where mid-day flex is present, core hours often need to be wide enough to allow both morning and afternoon meetings.

6. How will settlement periods be defined?

Employees on flexitime often work more or less hours than they have scheduled. Every so often, the discrepancy needs to be adjusted. The period between adjustments is called a "settlement period."

Longer settlement periods afford greater flexibility for employees but less management control over staff schedules. If debits and credits can be carried over from one settlement period, shorter settlement periods can provide both flexibility and more control. The usual practice is to make the settlement period equivalent to one pay period. The choices include:

flex-day. A one-day settlement period insures tight control but imposes severe limitations on the development of the flexitime concept.

flex-week. Extending the settlement period over one week allows employees more flexibility to cope with fluctuating work loads and personal responsibilities.

flex-month. A monthly accounting period allows a good deal of flexibility, particularly when debits and credits can be carried over to the next period.

flex-year. Some schemes are designed so that employees can work different hours at certain times of the year (longer hours in the winter and shorter hours in the summer, for example). The settlement period needn't be as long as a year to accomplish this if there are adequate carry over and hours banking provisions.

7. Will employees be able to bank extra hours?

In most programs, the employee's time sheet contains a running balance of surplus or deficit hours. There may be limits on how far employees can work ahead of or fall behind their salaried hours.

8. Will employees be able to take a full day off?

Most flexitime participants see the ability to take an occasional day off as a big attraction of the program. However, this is also the area that causes the most grief for employers. It has led to the cancellation of more than one flexitime program. The major problems are:

- inadequate staff coverage on Fridays, which are the most popular day off.
- employees who fail to give adequate warning of their intention to take a day off.
- difficulties in arranging meetings.

There are a number of ways to avoid these problems. Supervisors can a) insist that employees sign up for days off and b) place a limit on the number of employees who can be away on any given day. This serves the dual purpose of ensuring adequate coverage and keeping the supervisor informed.

Some organizations reserve a specific day of the week for meetings, and no time off is allowed on that day. In organizations where internal communication is more important than daily interaction with clients (some engineering or architectural firms, for instance), employees may be permitted to take a day off on, say, the first Friday of each month. This restricts the number of days on which a team member may be absent.

... I TAKE IT YOUR NEW HOURS ARE WORKING
OUT WELL, SANDUSKY...

Some organizations reserve a specific day of the week for meetings, and no time off is allowed on that day. In organizations where internal communication is more important than daily interaction with clients (some engineering or architectural firms, for instance), employees may be permitted to take a day off on, say, the first Friday of each month. This restricts the number of days on which a team member may be absent.

Any of these mechanisms can be successful; the important thing is to organize days off in a way that will minimize disruption.

9. What systems will facilitate communication between staff members?

Staff meetings should always be scheduled during core hours. It also helps to pick one day of the week for staff meetings. Employees should observe certain courtesies, like informing close co-workers before taking a day off or making any significant schedule changes.

10. How will employees maintain continuity with clients?

Some techniques for maintaining continuity with clients will develop spontaneously once flexitime is in place, but a couple of standard procedures are useful. One is the use of a designated alternate: "If you call back after 3 p.m., I won't be here, but Dwayne will be able to help you." Regular clients also deserve a courtesy call when any major schedule changes are on the way.

11. How will supervisors maintain control?

Managers may be concerned about the fact that employees on flexitime will often be working without direct supervision. Sometimes they are afraid that employees will cut corners or slack off if no one is around to police them. Leaving aside the question of whether or not this is a valid concern, how can a flexitime program be designed in a way that won't leave managers feeling that they have lost control?

One solution is to arrange for every manager to have a designated stand-in, usually someone who prefers to work earlier or later than the manager. The designated stand-in is cross trained to be able to do all or part of the manager's duties. The stand-in is kept informed about current issues and policies and also covers when the manager is on sick leave or vacation. This kind of back-up for management personnel is also a valuable form of "insurance" in case a manager leaves suddenly and a good way to train future managers.

12. What rules will ensure adequate staff coverage?

Flexitime can enable a company to extend its business hours. This is especially useful for companies that have a sales or service function; they can serve more clients between 7 a.m. and 6 p.m. than between 8 a.m. and 4 p.m. Some precautions are necessary, however. Suppose clients expect to be able to reach someone at 5:30 p.m. What happens if it's a beautiful Friday afternoon in July and everyone leaves promptly at 3 o'clock?

Some organizations designate a few people for early or late coverage in order to ensure that at least a skeleton staff is always on duty. Other organizations rotate responsibility for early and late coverage and for opening or closing the office. Some organizations make their official office hours shorter than the bandwidth; for instance, the office may be open from 8 a.m. to 5 p.m. even though some employees may start as early as 7 a.m. and others may work as late as 6 p.m.

13. How will your employer benefit from flexitime?

The best way to get approval for a flexitime program is to make sure it benefits the employer as well as the participants. Would longer business hours be an advantage to the company? Could flexitime help the company make more efficient use of some equipment? Does the company have a problem with lateness or absenteeism? Could flexitime help spread lunch breaks over a longer period and improve staff coverage at mid-day? Would flexitime help the company deal with peaks and valleys in its work load?

14. How will the program be implemented?

The following mechanisms are useful in the implementation process.

- *Hours of work committee*

This committee, made up of representatives from management and labour, develops all policies, decides who is eligible for the program, and conducts an ongoing evaluation.

• *Trial period*

A trial period or program in a single department may be useful in gaining approval from management.

• *Flexitime umpire*

The flexitime umpire should be someone with good mediation skills who is respected by both labour and management. The umpire may be called in if a manager wants to cancel flexitime for a specific position or if an employee claims to have been denied flexitime privileges unfairly or if any disagreement develops concerning the rules of the program.

• *Recording system*

It is necessary to record hours and keep track of credits and debits. Possibilities include the honor system, checklists, sign-in sheets, time clocks and personal time logs. A "Flextime Machine" has also been developed (the name is copyrighted). The device records the employee's accumulated hours rather than specific starting and quitting times.

• *Overtime policy*

The Labour Standards Branch of your provincial Ministry of Labour can tell you what the overtime rules are in your province. Most provinces allow employees and management to adjust overtime regulations if they make a joint application for an exemption.

Flexitime often requires bending the standard overtime rules. If employees want the opportunity to work nine hours on Monday and Tuesday in order to leave early on Wednesday afternoon, they can hardly expect their employer to pay overtime rates for the extra hours on Monday and Tuesday.

On the other hand, suppose an employee starts work at 7 a.m. and plans to leave at 3 p.m. What happens if the boss shows up at 2 o'clock with three more hours of "urgent" work? Should the employee be paid straight time or overtime for the hours between 3 and 5 p.m.? It is important to determine:

  ◦ what constitutes overtime.

  ◦ how overtime will be compensated.

- ° what options the employee will have concerning these questions.

- ° the limits within which a supervisor can ask for extra work or a change in an employee's schedule.

- ° what happens in the case of a dispute.

- *Adequate information*

Briefing materials that clearly define all aspects of a flexitime program will help reduce confusion and ease the implementation process.

 Compressed and Modified Work Weeks

The design for a compressed or modified work week should address the following questions. (Design considerations for staggered hours will be discussed separately.)

1. Who will be eligible for the program?

There are really two questions here, depending on the program design.

- *Who is allowed to participate?*
- *Who must participate?*

In a factory situation, the compressed work week is likely to disrupt operations unless all line positions and their supervisors are required to participate. However, support staff such as janitors, personnel managers, shipping clerks, switchboard operators, marketing personnel, security officers, accountants, etc. may be exempt.

It may be useful for some staff to remain on a standard schedule in order to deal with clients or outside suppliers. If the need for support services increases with the number of line staff on a modified work week, it may be necessary to restrict participation unless support workers agree to rotate their schedules in order to ensure adequate coverage.

2. How long will the work day run?

Several factors go into choosing the length of the work day. Employee preferences are obviously important. Work loads are also a factor: a shorter work day is better in situations where the work is strenuous or intense. However, longer shifts mean more days off.

The length of a shift should take account of peaks in demand, and shifts should fit together in a way that provides comprehensive coverage.

Popular choices are 7.5, 8, 8.75, 9, 9.5, 10, 12 and 12.5 hours. Although shifts of odd lengths such as eight hours and 53.33 minutes may add up to an even number of hours every two weeks, they are not a good idea. Case studies indicate that odd bits of time are often wasted because employees resent or ignore them. It makes more sense to change the hours in the work week in order to make the numbers come out even.

3. How will shifts fit together?

If several crews are needed to operate a factory or a hospital around the clock, shifts must be synchronized to provide the right pattern of coverage. Twelve-hour shifts give full 24-hour coverage, but many organizations can get by with two nine- or 10-hour shifts. Four-days-on/four-days-off schedules are popular. Continuous operation is also possible with a rotation of three-days-on/four-days-off/four-days-on/three-days-off.

4. How many hours will the work week contain?

The length of the work week is determined by the length of the shifts and the required pattern of coverage. Compressed work weeks of 35 or 36 hours cause fewer problems than 38- to 42-hour work weeks.

5. What days of the week will employees work?

Tuesday to Friday schedules make sense because they are seldom affected by statutory holidays. Employers are under no legal obligation to pay for a statutory holiday that falls on a nonscheduled work day. However, some do because of the convenience attached to a Tuesday to Friday schedule.

6. How will employees maintain continuity with clients and suppliers?

This is not a problem for facilities that operate continuously, but it does affect companies that operate with only one shift. One solution is to keep all or part of the sales and office staff on a standard five-day schedule. Another is to have part of the office staff and part of the security/maintenance staff on compressed schedules at opposite ends of the week.

7. What arrangements will be made to ensure a full service operation five days a week?

This question concerns companies that provide a direct service using only one shift of workers. The usual strategy is to divide the work force in half; one group works Monday to Thursday, and the other group works Tuesday to Friday. All staff must be cross-trained to help with customer service and take a front-line position if necessary. (In case studies of the compressed work week, participants often say that taking on more varied duties makes their jobs more interesting and challenging.) Some organizations bolster their Monday and Friday coverage by asking for volunteers who prefer to take their day off mid-week.

8. How will the program benefit your employer?

A compressed work week can be designed to provide extended business hours or better coverage of peak hours. It may also reduce overtime and cut the time devoted to start-up and shut-down operations. The design of the program should incorporate some practical benefits that will help sell the employer on the idea.

9. How will the program be implemented?

Four mechanisms are helpful in implementing a compressed work week program.

- *Hours of work committee*

This committee, made up of representatives from management and labour, will help with the final design and will also monitor, refine and evaluate the program.

- *Needs survey of potential participants*

Case studies show that employees feel more positive about programs if they have some say in their design.

- *Written overtime policy*

If the standard work day exceeds eight hours, you will need to consult with the Labour Standards Branch of your provincial Ministry of Labour. Exemptions from overtime regulations can usually be arranged. If the standard work week is less than 40 hours, it is important to decide when overtime rates apply.

- *Trial period*

The trial period should be long enough to give workers time to adjust to the new schedule before evaluation begins.

Designing a Staggered Hours Program

The staggered hours approach often works best for a facility that operates continuously. The following steps are useful in designing a staggered hours program.

1. Establish an hours of work committee with representatives from management and labour.

2. Conduct an informal poll of employees to establish the range of preferred starting times for the various shifts.

3. Conduct a formal survey that asks employees to choose a starting time from a range of possible options.

4. Collate the results of the survey and design new "matched" shifts that will provide continuous coverage. Employees whose choice cannot be accommodated will remain on the old starting time.

5. Develop a policy for new employees. New employees should be assigned a starting time, but they can request a change when an opening occurs on a preferred shift.

6. Develop a system for staggering shifts before and after a temporary shut down.

7. Develop a policy for overtime rates and relief staffing to take account of the new shift schedules.

Businesses that do not operate continuously may also benefit from staggered hours if they need fewer staff at the beginning or end of the day. This situation is often a good opportunity for an individual or a small group of employees to propose a system of staggered hours. The design of such a system needs:

- a plan to deal with your duties during the business hours before or after your shift begins or ends. You may be able to arrange for someone on regular hours to cover for you if necessary.
- a plan for arranging your duties in a way that benefits your employer. You may be able to help with start-up or shut-down procedures, offer extended hours of service or handle special orders. You may need to change your duties slightly if you want to start earlier or later than everyone else.

Home Work / Telecommuting

The success of home work arrangements depends as much on the personality of the job holder as on the nature of the position. For this reason, designs for telecommuting arrangements are highly individualized.

The following questions will help you design a plan for working at home.

1. What tasks are you responsible for?

Make a list of your duties. Include informal, incidental and occasional duties as well as regular tasks. (You may be the unofficial fix-it person for the office or the resident expert on something; you may be asked to draw a poster occasionally.) Next to each item on your list, mark an "H" if you could do the task at home without special equipment; "E" if you could do the task at home given the proper equipment, and "O" if you need to do the task at the office.

2. How much of the time will you work at home?

If your list contains only a few "H"s and "E"s, occasional afternoons at home would make sense. But if your list contains mostly "H"s and "E"s and if you can find a way to delegate the "O"s to someone else, you may be able to work at home full-time. Working at home full-time may be too isolating, however. How much contact do you need with other people? How much time can you spend away from the office without feeling out of touch or invisible? What balance between home and office would you prefer?

3. When will you work at home?

Are there certain days of the week when it would be less disruptive for you to work away from the office? Should you work at home only part of the day? Perhaps you would prefer the freedom to work at home periodically as the need arises. Would you plan to be "on duty" at home during your regular office hours? Or do you want the choice of working during the evenings or weekends?

4. Who will cover for you when you're away from the office?

Do you need to be "on call" for jobs that can't be postponed or handled over the phone? Who else could do those jobs for you? Will someone in the office handle your phone calls? How can you structure your activities to make life easier for the person who covers for you? (Keeping your files up to date and in good order would be one example. Letting major clients know when you plan to be away from the office would be another.)

5. What equipment will you need?

Technology can make it easier for you to work at home, but there may be some extra expense involved. Will you need an extra phone line into your home or is your residential line sufficient? Would it help to add a "call waiting" alert to your phone service? Does your office phone system permit conference calls? Can the switchboard patch calls through to you directly? (Your clients don't have to know you are at home.)

What computer equipment will you need? Is a modem necessary? Is a printer necessary? Is a FAX machine necessary to send material that is available only in hard copy or would occasional use of a courier service be cheaper? Who will pay for computer equipment in your home? If you buy it, will your employer pay a fee for the use of your machine?

6. How can you make your home work space comfortable?

A room that was adequate as a den or study may not be suitable for a work space that you will use for several hours at a time. Is the lighting adequate? Is your chair comfortable? If you are working at a computer, the keyboard and monitor should be at the right height to avoid straining your neck. Do you have privacy from the rest of the house? How permeable is the room to sound?

If you are in a full telecommuting arrangement, all of these concerns are especially important. If your employer doesn't need a work space for you at the office, you may be able to finance improvements by charging rent for your home office.

7. How can you keep the level of distractions manageable?

Do you need to enroll your school age children in an after school program or a summer camp? Will your spouse leave you alone to work? If young children will be in the house, can you control the noise level?

8. How can you keep in touch with your work mates?

The more you work at home, the more carefully you should think about this question. It's easy to dismiss work relationships as unimportant until you have to do without them. Attending staff meetings, serving on project committees, checking in by phone, attending work-related social events and volunteering for union duties can all help maintain the human connection in your work. If you keep in touch with people at work, you'll have more influence on policy decisions, you'll be more visible at promotion time and you'll have more allies if you find yourself the victim of office politics.

9. How will you implement your home work program?

A number of mechanisms may be helpful. One is a trial period. A written agreement can also be useful, particularly for full telecommuting. The agreement should spell out the conditions of your home work arrangement. It should state explicitly that working at home will not alter your seniority or job status, and it should include a contingency plan in case the telecommuting arrangement is cancelled. You may have to devise an alternate method of recording your hours. Finally, make sure that your home insurance policy will cover your office equipment, particularly if your employer owns it.

10. What policies are needed?

If you are telecommuting from a satellite centre, you may need a policy framework that establishes general procedures and protections. An hours of work committee with representatives from labour and management is a useful mechanism. The committee would establish telecommuting policies and mediate any problems that arise. In particular, the committee can look at eligibility criteria, an application process, equipment policies (who pays for what), a needs survey and job protection.

Step Six

Getting What You Want

Planning Strategy

If you are lucky, you have the kind of sensitive, progressive employer who knows that satisfied employees are productive employees. In that case, you shouldn't have too much trouble getting a flexible work schedule that includes fair treatment on wages and benefits.

However, most people have to do some negotiating to get the flexible schedule they want. Negotiation works, and thousands of Canadian workers have done it successfully, but it requires careful planning, good strategy and self-confidence. In the words of the *I Ching,* you must "pull the tail of the tiger with great humor."

Who Is On Your Side?

The first step in negotiating is to do some research. Find allies, and identify obstacles. Identify the needs and values in your work place that will help or hinder you. Start by taking an inventory of your strengths.

- *Are your skills and experience valuable to your employer?* ( )

- *Are you a good worker?* ( )

- *Do you have a good relationship with your supervisor?* ( )

- *Does your employer want to be seen as progressive* ( ) *innovative* ( ) *fair* ( ) *efficient and/or caring?* ( )

- *Do you have a good relationship with your union representative?* ( )

- *Is the personnel department concerned about employee morale?* ( )

- *Do you have other options if your employer won't give you what you want?* ( )

- *Is your union likely to be supportive?* ( )

Check marks indicate strengths you can use in negotiating for what you want. (If you don't have any checks, are you sure you want to work there? Maybe you should be looking for another job.) Remember these strengths when it comes time to make a proposal to your employer. If your employer likes to be seen as fair-minded, make your request on the grounds of fairness. If your employer values efficiency, argue that your new work schedule is more efficient. Now look at the obstacles you face.

- *Would you be easy to replace?* ( )

- *Is your supervisor unsupportive or unsympathetic to your needs?* ( )

- *Is your supervisor too busy to consider making changes?* ( )

- *Does your employer take an "if-you-don't-like-it-you-can-leave" attitude?* ( )

- *Is your employer slow to implement new ideas?* ( )

- *Does the personnel department do things "by the book?"* ( )

- *Is your union unsympathetic or hostile to new work arrangements?* ( )

This kind of an inventory will give you an idea of where you should tread cautiously and who to enlist as an ally. If you can see that you have little leverage with your employer and a lot of inertia working against you, don't lose heart. The Quakers have an expression: "Speaking truth to power." If you ask for something that is fair and reasonable and you persist in asking, the system will often give you what you want in the end. You may not have a lot of power, but never underestimate the effectiveness of a quiet truth.

How Can You Improve Your Chances?

A well-organized written proposal is a powerful tool for getting what you want. There are several reasons why written (or more accurately, typed) proposals have a much better chance of approval than oral requests.

The process of writing a proposal helps you get your plan clear in your own mind. Writing things down is the best way of organizing the

DAUNTING, ISN'T IT...?

details of your new schedule and making sure you have covered all the angles.

Supervisors often turn down requests for new work schedules because they imagine things that could go wrong. If a written proposal takes account of potential problems and suggests some solutions, the new arrangement cannot be dismissed out of hand.

Supervisors usually have a lot to do. When you present a carefully designed plan for a new work schedule, your employer doesn't have to do much work in order to say "yes."

A written proposal is harder to ignore. Employers often ignore verbal requests for new work schedules. A solid and substantial written proposal shows that you are serious and that a definite response is required.

Proposals often require approval from two or three levels of administration. A written proposal is the most effective way to carry your case to the upper levels. It gives your supervisor a justification for pushing your application forward: "I have a written request from an employee that requires some sort of response."

When you design the playing field, you have a better chance of controlling the game. If you create a reasonable framework for your new work schedule, including a suggested benefit package, your employer is likely to accept your suggestions as they stand.

For all these reasons, a written proposal is far more effective than an oral request. Oral requests have, at the most, a 25 per cent chance of approval, but the odds in favor of a written proposal are considerably better than even.

Who Should Make the Proposal?

There are three ways to make a proposal.

- You can submit a proposal as an **individual**.
- You can find some like-minded co-workers and submit a **group** proposal.
- You can persuade your **union** to make a proposal.

Let's look at each of these alternatives in turn.

INDIVIDUAL PROPOSALS

Organizations do not like to change their policies on hours of work. Like individuals, organizations dislike major changes. It's usually much easier to convince them to make an exception for one person or to approve something on a trial basis.

When only one person is involved, the stakes are relatively small. If you have a well-designed plan that doesn't require a change in financial benefits that would set a precedent for other employees, you can often get approval from your immediate supervisor without involving the upper levels of the administration. This is the quickest and easiest route because the time and effort needed for approval goes up exponentially the more people are involved.

Sometimes you can get special treatment on benefits if you can show that your situation is unique in some way and will not set a precedent for others. For example, if you are the only person in your organization with a particular set of duties, other employees wouldn't necessarily be involved if you get permission for flexitime or a compressed work week. Your employer may be reluctant to agree to a policy of phased retirement at full pay, but if you have a unique personal reason for making such a request—severe heart trouble, for instance, or a spouse who is suffering from Alzheimer's disease—your employer can justify making a special arrangement in your case.

Organizations rarely make job sharing, permanent part-time, leaves of absence or telecommuting available as a matter of policy unless they have had some previous experience with individual arrangements. If no one in your work place has ever tried these options, your best chance is to ask your employer to make an exception for you. Organizations usually watch to see how several such experiments work out before changing their personnel policy.

Phased retirement, compressed work weeks, flexitime, V-Time and banked overtime all tend to require changes to the payroll structure. For that reason, individuals are rarely successful in getting approval for these arrangements unless they can claim special circumstances (a chronic health problem, for example) or present a design that minimizes structural changes.

As a general rule, individual proposals tend to have less force than union proposals. The other point to remember is that individuals have limited means of protecting their rights if a supervisor tries to change or undermine the arrangement. Unions can invoke grievance procedures to protect your rights if they have negotiated the work option program as part of the collective bargaining process.

GROUP PROPOSALS

Organizing a group proposal takes time and energy, and you may have to compromise on what you want. An organized group, particularly if it's a large one, may put some employers on their guard.

On the other hand, employers will sometimes accept a request from a group that they wouldn't accept from an individual. For example, an employer is more likely to change the pension plan if a dozen employees ask to phase into retirement than if one employee requests it. A joint job sharing proposal from six employees may send a stronger signal to an employer than a request from a single individual.

In general, group proposals are better at getting an employer's attention. Groups have more bargaining power than individuals, and they are more effective in lobbying for changes to policy or personnel structures. If the work schedule you want requires such changes and you don't have a union (or your union is unhelpful), a group proposal is probably your best bet. This is almost always true for V-Time, banked overtime and compensatory benefit leaves; and it's usually the case with flexitime, compressed work weeks and phased retirement.

UNION PROPOSALS

Depending on the politics of your work place, getting your union involved can either help or hurt your proposal. If your union is strong, has a good working relationship with management, or is supportive of flexible work schedules, a union proposal may be the most effective approach. If your union is weak and ineffectual, if it adopts a confrontational style in its dealings with management or if the leadership is hostile to flexible work schedules, union involvement probably won't help your cause.

Unions don't always have to be in agreement with your ideas to be of assistance, however. For instance, the Canadian Union of Public Employees (CUPE) opposes the principle of job sharing, but the union has negotiated job sharing arrangements for members on several occasions.

Unions can be effective in negotiating any of the work options described in Step Two. However, union participation is usually essential in negotiating any arrangement that involves paid time off: for example, paid educational leave, paid parental leave, paid phased retirement and so on.

It will not always be clear whether an individual proposal, a group proposal or a union proposal has the best chance of success. In many cases, all you can do is make your best guess and cross your fingers.

If you are writing your own proposal to deal with an isolated situation, use the format in the next chapter. If you want to set up a work option program that would be available to a group of individuals or to all members of a bargaining unit, skip ahead to "Writing a Collective Proposal."

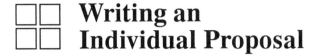

Writing an Individual Proposal

Writing a proposal may seem overwhelming, but it is not so difficult if you take it one step at a time. You don't have to create a masterpiece of logic and persuasion: just think out a design carefully and write it up in an organized fashion. Be concise: your final proposal should not be more than three to five (typed) pages. If our format doesn't fit your style (or your organization), modify it accordingly. If the chain of command that needs to approve your proposal is short, i.e., you work for a small organization or your immediate supervisor has sufficient authority to approve your request directly, your proposal can be less detailed and less formal than when head office approval is required.

One last piece of advice: a proposal should propose, not threaten. Don't say something like "If you don't give me what I am asking for in this proposal, I intend to quit." That's more likely to offend your employer than increase your bargaining power. If you are bluffing, you will probably regret it. If your bottom line is a firm decision to leave if you don't get a better work arrangement, wait until you have exhausted all other avenues of persuasion before raising that possibility.

All individual proposals should have the following elements.

1. Introduction

Begin with a short statement of purpose that outlines in a sentence or two the bare bones of what you want: "I, John Thomas, marketing manager of the Agribiz Division, propose to share my position with Harvey Shuster on a six-month trial basis, as outlined below. "

2. Job description

Draw up a detailed description of your job or use your official job description. In either case, include the following information:

- job title.
- status.
- location.
- department.

- supervisor.
- a brief summary of your duties (25 words or less).
- responsibilities and accountabilities — what (and who) are you in charge of?
- job specifications — what are your specific duties?

  ◦ *What tasks do you do on your own?*

  ◦ *How often do you supervise others?*

  ◦ *Do you work with confidential information?*

  ◦ *Do you handle cash?*

  ◦ *How complex are your job tasks?*

  ◦ *How much do you interact with the public and other staff?*

  ◦ *What are the education requirements of your job?*

  ◦ *How much experience or training does your job require?*

This level of detail may seem unnecessary since your immediate supervisor probably has the information already, but include it anyway. Your proposal may need the approval of someone in personnel or upper management who knows nothing about you or your situation.

3. Backfill coverage/redefinition of duties

If you are not changing anything but your place of work or the arrangement of your hours (telecommuting, flexitime, compressed work week), this section is unnecessary. On the other hand, if you want to work fewer hours, you need to describe a means of dealing with the work you won't be able to handle yourself. At the very least, you need to suggest a framework for covering your duties. For example, a nurse who proposes to go on a four-day work week might say, "A part-time relief person should be hired on a contract basis to work every Friday."

In many cases, however, it helps to suggest a specific person who could fill in for you. Management is less likely to object to your proposal if accepting it doesn't involve the trouble of recruiting qualified or trained staff. By suggesting a specific person whom you know is qualified and with whom you feel comfortable, you also reduce the odds of being forced to work with someone who may cause you grief.

In your proposal, briefly outline the skills of the suggested fill-in person, including:

- experience.
- education.
- abilities.
- a brief description of how the person's skills match and complement yours.
- an outline of the training or orientation the fill-in person will need.
- a copy of the person's resume as an appendix to your proposal.

What if you are unable to locate an appropriate fill-in person but you expect to be working very closely with that person (job sharing, phased retirement, for example)? In that case, you might want to include a provision in your proposal that will assure you a role in the selection process. You could include a statement such as, "The position will be advertised in the local newspaper and applicants will be screened by a hiring committee made up of the personnel manager, myself and my immediate supervisor."

If someone else will be doing part of your job, how will the work be divided? Does the work divide tidily into separate tasks or will you need to develop a process for sharing some tasks?

Explain your rationale for splitting the job in a certain way: for example, "Because of her greater accounting experience, my partner Janice would handle bookkeeping. I would maintain continuity with customers by continuing to make all sales calls."

State clearly in your proposal whether your fill-in person will be taking full responsibility for a particular area of work or whether you will retain overall responsibility with the fill-in person occupying the role of an assistant. Indicate whether you want to have your work performance evaluated separately or as a team.

4. Time schedules

Describe your proposed work schedule in precise detail. If a fill-in person (or a job sharing partner) is covering part of your work, describe that person's schedule in equal detail.

Think about whether you and your fill-in partner will require overlapping schedules in order to trade information. Do you want the right to trade time on occasion? (This question is most germane for job sharing partners, but it might also apply to phased retirement, permanent part-time and leaves of absence.) What special arrangements will apply in regard to staff meetings, statutory holidays and vacation time?

5. Continuity/communication concerns

If you will be rearranging your work hours (flexitime, compressed work week), changing your work place (telecommuting) or reducing your hours (all the other options), you need to describe a workable plan for minimizing disruptions to work continuity and information flow. What information could get lost in the shuffle? How will you pass on important information from customers, clients, supervisors and staff meetings?

In this section, list all the potential continuity/communication problems that could develop as a result of your new schedule. Either design a mechanism to deal with the problem or show how the current system deals with it adequately. The following areas may need some comment:

staff meetings/staff memos.

schedule postings. How will others know when you're in or out?

urgent calls or crisis situations.

front-line coverage. Are you "on call" for any duties?

unfinished tasks and follow up. How will you complete unfinished business or hand it over to fill-in staff?

client continuity. If you are not always available, how can you make sure your clients feel they are getting consistent service?

information exchange. How will you exchange important information with your job sharing partner or fill-in staff?

This is a key section in your proposal. You must try to forestall objections from your employer by providing solutions for all the potential communications and continuity problems in your proposal. It will be harder for your employer to turn you down if you have dealt with all the problems in advance.

6. Suggested benefit package

Flexitime, telecommuting, compressed work weeks and banked overtime have no effect on benefit packages because they involve the standard number of working hours. However, anyone proposing a compressed work week must specify a mechanism for dealing with statutory holidays.

People who want short-term leave (less than 90 days), paid leave, phased retirement or cuts in work time of 10 per cent or less can ask for full fringe benefits. Older workers should also deal with the question of pension plan contributions: for example, "Contributions to the pension plan will continue at the normal rate for full-time employment."

For options not mentioned above, the best strategy is to ask for a benefit package that is prorated according to the number of hours worked. Prorated benefits add to the persuasiveness of your proposal because they have little or no effect on an employer's payroll costs. At the same time, employees who get prorated benefits have a better deal than most casual part-time staff. (See "The Politics of Benefits," page 110.)

In this section, you need to list all your present benefits and indicate how they will be affected by your proposal. It also helps to introduce this section with a short statement of principle: "Fringe benefits are a part of an employee's total wage package, and any employee on reduced hours deserves an approximately proportionate share of benefits or a cash payment in lieu of partial benefits."

To understand how your present benefit package will be affected, circle the appropriate categories below. (You may also want to see "What will Happen to Your Benefits" in Step Four.) If you are not sure whether or not you receive a specific benefit, check with your union steward or your personnel manager.

- *Unemployment Insurance, Canada Pension Plan and Worker's Compensation*

UIC, CPP (or QPP) and Worker's Compensation contributions are all based on a percentage of income. In your proposal, you can simply say, "UIC, CPP and Worker's Compensation prorate automatically when income is reduced."

- *Vacation and sick leave*

Vacation and sick leave will normally be "prorated as a proportion of the normal full-time allotment."

● *Statutory holidays*

Statutory holidays can be prorated — although sometimes with difficulty. If you are proposing a shorter work day, "statutory holidays prorate automatically." If you are proposing a shorter work year, there would normally be "no payment for statutory holidays that fall during time off."

If you are proposing a shorter work week, the mechanics of prorating statutory holidays can be extremely complicated. The simplest method is to say that "If a statutory holiday falls on a scheduled work day, the employee will receive payment for the number of hours the employee would be expected to work." If you work most Mondays, you will come out ahead by this arrangement; if not, you will be somewhat penalized. (Job sharers often trade schedules in order to apportion statutory holidays fairly.)

The other alternative is to say that "All statutory holidays will be prorated." In that case, if you work three-quarters time, you would get three-quarters of a day's pay for each statutory holiday whether you were scheduled to work that day or not. This approach is fairer, but it tends to cause fluctuations in your paycheques. They are smaller when a statutory holiday falls on a scheduled work day and larger if it falls on a day when you are not scheduled to work. Sometimes, employees arrange to adjust their work hours in weeks that contain a statutory holiday in order to equalize paycheques.

The following items refer to supplementary benefits. Unlike the previous statutory benefits, most supplementary benefits are difficult, if not impossible, to prorate. The usual solution is to alter the whole package of supplementary benefits in a way that reduces the cost by the same percentage as the reduction in your work hours. For example, if your work hours are reduced by 25 per cent, you should find ways to cut the overall cost of your supplementary benefits by one-quarter. Try to retain the most important benefits or those that would be more expensive if you purchased them privately.

If you ask your union or the personnel department for the exact cost of each of your supplementary benefits, you will be able to divide the package fairly accurately; otherwise you will have to make a rough estimate and negotiate the final details later.

- *Registered Retirement Savings Plans*

RRSPs can be purchased privately for about the same price.

- *Company pension plans*

Company pension plans vary greatly in their structure and the basis for calculating pension income. Some pension plans are administered by the employer, and others are administered by an outside pension fund. Changing the rules is a lot harder in the latter case.

Some plans base pensions on lifetime earnings; in that case, working less for a few years has a relatively small effect, even if those years are your final years of employment. In some plans, earnings in the last five years of employment have a big effect on pension income, regardless of years of service. In that case, you probably won't be able to afford to work less prior to retirement without negotiating a change in the pension plan.

Some plans base pensions on the level of contributions to the plan. In that case, you can reduce your work hours with absolutely no effect on your pension so long as you and/or your employer continue to make contributions as though you were working full-time.

Some plans will disqualify you if you work less than full-time. Others allow you to prorate your length of service: for example, every year of half-time work is equivalent to six months of full-time service.

Ask your union steward or the personnel office for information about your pension plan and the effect of reducing your work hours. You can often use the official wording to describe the arrangement you prefer. If you can't find out what your options are (or you don't understand them), it is often wise to say, "This proposal is contingent on arrangements for pension contributions that will not adversely affect my future pension."

One other idea about pensions: if you are not planning to stay with your current employer for a long time (ten years or more, for instance), you may not qualify for a pension. In that case, you may as well trade your pension benefit for the chance to retain full medical and dental insurance. (You should also be looking at starting a private Registered Retirement Savings Plan.)

- *Provincial medical insurance premiums*

Provincial medical insurance premiums can be dealt with in a number of ways. If you are covered by your spouse's medical insurance, you can trade medical coverage for a full benefit elsewhere. If not, you can pay all or part of the cost of your medical insurance premiums yourself as a payroll deduction. You can drop coverage through your employer and pay privately, or you can ask to retain full medical insurance in exchange for waiving other benefits.

- *Dental insurance plans*

Dental insurance plans are expensive to buy privately, so unless you are covered under your spouse's plan, you should keep your dental plan benefit. If you don't have other benefits to "trade," you can offer to pay part of the cost as a payroll deduction.

- *Extended medical insurance*

Extended medical insurance is also expensive to buy privately. Don't trade it unless you are covered under your spouse's plan.

- *Group life, disability insurance and short-term illness insurance plans*

These are normally based on a percentage of salary, so they "prorate automatically according to income." However, some plans have rules that exclude part-time employees. In other plans, the rules will allow you to continue contributing as though you were working full-time.

- *Profit-sharing plans*

Profit-sharing dividends are usually received as a percentage of income, so they also "prorate automatically."

- *Other benefits*

Other benefits may include stock options, health club memberships, Employee Assistance Plan services, etc. These are unusual, and although they may be valuable to you as an employee, they are often hard to evaluate in hard figures. Don't bother trying to set a price on them, and don't mention them in your proposal.

If working on the benefits section of your proposal makes you feel a) confused b) hysterical c) overwhelmed or d) hopeless, don't be alarmed. That's only to be expected. Do the best you can, and go on to the next section. The personnel department will have to handle anything you can't deal with.

7. Costs

Employers often fear that nonstandard work schedules will cost them money. Itemizing costs and potential savings usually makes it clear that the expense involved is manageable. The following costs are worth considering.

- If your proposal involves adding another part-time position, the cost in paperwork will be approximately $100 per year.
- If you are asking to retain full benefits, itemize the benefits and, if possible, indicate the cost. (The personnel manager and your union financial agent should both have this information.)
- When positions with a salary significantly over $25,000 per year are reduced in hours and backfilled, it results in "a slight increase in employer UIC, CPP and Worker's Compensation payments due to the effect of contribution ceilings." (No extra cost is incurred if the salary is $25,000 or under.)
- If your proposal requires extra office space, staff training, extra staff meetings or overlap time, list them as costs with an estimated dollar value, if possible.
- List any rental expenses (special equipment, etc.).

The following areas are sources of possible savings.

- If your proposal involves hiring a less experienced employee, the wage package may be less than yours. (This situation occurs most frequently in phased retirement programs.)
- Using part-time employees may mean that your employer has to pay less overtime. If you know how much overtime an average full-time employee works you can often attach a dollar value to these savings.
- If your organization already has part-time staff and keeps records on absenteeism, you can make a dollar estimate of the expected savings resulting from reduced absenteeism.

Your proposal should take account of the following start-up costs:

- the cost of hiring and training fill-in staff.
- the cost of purchasing extra equipment.
- the time personnel department staff will spend designing and implementing the program.

Try to collect enough hard numbers to make a clear statement such as: "This job sharing arrangement will have an estimated net cost of $600 per year, primarily in increased benefit costs." It's also a good idea to mention aspects of the proposal that will avoid additional costs: "Because my proposed job sharing partner has recently retired from a similar position, training costs will be minimal."

8. Advantages and disadvantages

List all the possible advantages and disadvantages that your work option will create for your employer. Mention any concerns that you have dealt with in the design of your program: "A clear division of duties and weekly cross-over meetings will minimize the possibility that one of the partners may overlook some task."

Possible advantages include:

- reduced absenteeism.
- reduced staff turnover.
- improved morale.
- increased productivity.
- better peak coverage.
- extended hours coverage.
- lunch hour/holiday/vacation coverage.
- emergency/overtime coverage.
- extra skills/specialized skills.
- health and safety benefits.
- cost savings.

Possible problem areas include:

- continuity.
- communication.
- staff meetings/staff training.
- supervision.
- uneven skill levels.
- co-worker attitudes.
- scheduling confusion.
- extra costs.

Try to be even-handed in assessing advantages and disadvantages. Work options should not be presented as a panacea, but rather as a workable trade-off in which the advantages outweigh the problems. (Note: in some proposals, "Advantages and disadvantages," called "Rationale," will fit best immediately after the Introduction.)

9. Local examples

Your case will be stronger if you can mention other employers who have had success with the system you are proposing. It helps if you can find examples which are a) fairly local, b) in the same occupational area and c) in the same industry. For example, a policeman who wants to work permanent part-time should make a point of mentioning the fact that the police officers in a nearby community are already working permanent part-time (particularly if the police chief thinks the program is a success).

Question your professional acquaintances and your union; make a few discreet calls to the personnel departments of other organizations. You may be able to uncover an example that will strengthen your case and perhaps give you some good ideas to use in the design of your own proposal.

10. A plan for implementation

A plan for implementation should include:

- a suggested starting date.
- a suggested trial period.
- suggested procedures for finalizing details of the new arrangement.

A suggested starting date reminds management about the need to make a decision. A trial period protects both you and your employer; it allows both parties to test the arrangement without making an irrevocable decision.

Procedures for finalizing the arrangement can be simple: "In consultation with the personnel department, my supervisor and I will draw up a written agreement outlining the specific details of the arrangement. This agreement will not come into force until it has been approved by both the personnel manager and my department head."

This kind of approach indicates that you will continue to be involved in the design process. It also keeps decisions close to home, assigns responsibility for the task and assures you the protection of a written agreement.

For a more concrete idea of what a work option proposal involves, take a look at the sample proposal on the next page.

TO: Jim Gordell, Manager, Driver Registration
Ministry of Transport, Sidney, B.C.
FROM: Sharon Belz and Jocelyn Wain
DATE: February 3, 1987
SUBJECT: Job Sharing Proposal

We, Sharon Belz and Jocelyn Wain, would like you to consider our proposal to share one of our keypunch operator positions.

Job Description: Our jobs are classified as KP02. We work at the Royal Avenue office, Driver Registration Department, Ministry of Transport, Sidney. Our immediate supervisor is Helene Smyth.

Duties: Our duties include using a Wang computer system to enter motor vehicle data such as accident reports, speeding tickets, name and address additions, changes and renewals, plus other vehicle-related documents. We do our work independently and in systematic order; each item is logged and checked. Other duties may include some clerical work.

Task Analysis: We have both worked in the same offices doing the same work for approximately seven years. We know our jobs well and feel that sharing our duties would be easy. The keypunch operator job lends itself to sharing because the tasks are not complex and require little communication. The current procedure is to log all incomplete tasks at the end of a shift. This makes changeover with a partner very easy. We both know all the aspects of our job and feel confident with each other as work partners. We have no hesitation in starting or completing one another's work and taking responsibility for any task.

Backfill Coverage: Any one of a number of former employees of the department could be rehired to fill the position that would open up when the two of us share one of our jobs. This person should be hired on a contract basis until the end of a trial period.

Time Schedules: We would like to share the work week by working one-week-on/one-week-off, changing over on Wednesdays. A calendar of our proposed 1987 work schedule is enclosed. If for any reason one of us needs more than one week off, we would like to be able to trade

Job Sharing Proposal. Page 2.

time. We would have to reach agreement with our supervisor before any time could be traded. We feel that this would be a good schedule; it would be simple to follow and everyone would know which partner was working on a particular day.

Communications: Any important information to be passed on, such as changes or updates, would be kept in a specific file. Our job does not require a lot of communication about the work in progress, but if necessary a phone call can be made for clarification. A calendar of the days when we would be working would be given to our supervisor and to Payroll so both would know when we were working. We would also give advance notice of any change in our schedules.

Benefits: Statutory benefits (Unemployment Insurance, Canada Pension and Worker's Compensation) would automatically be prorated. Compensatory benefits (sick leave, statutory holidays and vacation time) would be divided in half. Jocelyn, who now gets 20 days vacation per year, would get 10; Sharon now has 15 days and would get seven and a half. Maternity leave remains the same. We would like to have the option for one partner to work full-time for the duration of the other's maternity leave. (This would mean the department would not have to find a replacement.)

If one of us is sick, the other partner could cover for that sick day so no time is lost to the employer. The sick person would then in turn take a day to work for the partner. Under our union contract the supplementary benefits (Medical Services Plan premiums, dental plan, extended medical, short-term illness protection, group life insurance and pension plan) are paid by the employer. Our pensions would be prorated. We wish to keep our seniority as calendar seniority.

Cost: Costs to the employer would be minor. Our salaries are the same; no extra cost there. Statutory and compensatory benefits prorate; no extra cost. There would be extra costs in carrying a second set of supplementary benefits (about $800/year), but these could be off-set by sick time coverage. Other special leaves for dentist, doctor and specialists' appointments would be almost nil because they could be arranged on time off. There is a small paperwork cost in keeping an

Job Sharing Proposal. Page 3.

extra employee on the payroll. There would be no cost to the employer for training, equipment or supervision. We would be sharing the same work space. If either of us worked extra hours, it would be at straight-time pay, which would be a cost benefit to the employer.

Advantages: Sharing our job would be good for us and the department. We feel at this time that part-time work would be more appropriate for our family lives and would also leave room for a more enthusiastic approach to our work. We could do our work with fewer fatigue-related mistakes. There would be lower absenteeism because the fill-in system could be implemented. If there is an overload of work, we could come in and help on our days off. This would alleviate stress with deadlines and would help the employer as well as fellow employees. The department would keep two valuable employees who know their job well and enjoy their work; two people would be available to give helpful input and ideas. A former employee of the department could be recalled from lay-off to fill the one vacant full-time position. Our supervisor seems agreeable and believes this job arrangement would work well. A letter of recommendation is attached.

Other Examples of Job Sharing: There are job shared positions in several government departments: Ministry of Finance, Office of the Comptroller General, Revenue, the Purchasing Commission and the Provincial Treasury. There are clerks, accountants and system analysts who job share. There seem to be positive feelings and results wherever it has been tried.

Implementation: To begin our job sharing, we would suggest a starting date of May 1, 1987. We would like to have a trial period of six months to see how the situation works out. At the end of six months, either side could terminate the arrangement if it is not to their satisfaction. If the arrangement were terminated at the end of the trial period, each of us would return to full-time, and the contract staff person would be laid off. We hope to continue job sharing for quite a few years, but should one of us leave, the remaining partner would like to have the option of returning to full-time.

Job Sharing Proposal. Page 4.

Once details of the arrangement are finalized, a written agreement would be drawn up so that both sides would be clear about the terms of the arrangement.

Thank you for your time and your consideration of this proposal. Sharon and I both feel positive that job sharing will work in our situation, and we are looking forward to receiving your answer.

Two attachments enclosed

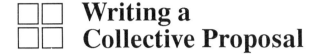

Writing a Collective Proposal

If several employees all want the same work option, they will need to draft an extensive written proposal, whether they are negotiating directly with management or through their union.

Collective proposals usually require the following ten elements.

1. Introduction

Begin with a short statement of purpose that outlines the objective in a sentence or two: "This proposal recommends the establishment of a trial job sharing program for Clerks 1 and 2 in the Health Services Branch."

2. Eligibility criteria

This section usually includes:

- *eligible classes of employee.*

Eligibility may be defined on the basis of occupation unit, age or length of service. Sometimes the criteria for eligibility changes according to the complexity of the job: "All Health Care Workers 1 and 2 with one year or more of service could be eligible for the program. Health Care Workers 3 and 4 would require the permission of their immediate supervisor and the Personnel Committee in order to be eligible."

Sometimes there are two levels of eligibility: "This phased retirement option would be available to any employee age 60 or over with 15 or more years of service and to any employee 55 and over with 20 or more years of service."

- *quotas.*

Many programs limit the number of participants: "In order to maintain continuity, no more than 25 per cent of the service representatives in any department would be allowed to job share."

- *an approval process.*

How will employees apply to participate in the program? "Employees would make written application to the Personnel Manager, who would be in charge of confirming their eligibility and securing the necessary approvals."

- *a veto clause.*

Many programs give either the department head or the participant's immediate supervisor the right to veto an individual's participation, either temporarily or permanently: "The department head may refuse entry into the program for any employee, either temporarily or indefinitely, if operational considerations make that employee's participation impractical. If an employee is refused entry to the program the department head must provide that employee with a written rationale outlining the reasons for refusal." (Escape clauses are a mixed blessing; management is more likely to approve the whole program if they have the right to say "no" in certain instances, but veto clauses can also be abused by inflexible managers.)

- *a redress procedure.*

Sometimes protection against abuse of the veto clause can be built into the program. "Employees who feel that they have been denied access to the program unfairly can file a grievance with the flexitime umpire."

- *an outsider clause.*

The language of such a clause might read as follows: "Employees not normally eligible for the program may apply for inclusion. Such instances will be decided on a case-by-case basis, at the discretion of the department head."

3. Backfill coverage/redefinition of duties

(This section is not necessary for flexitime, compressed work week and telecommuting proposals.) Several decisions must be made if employees will be reducing their work hours.

- How will participating employees' duties be reassigned, shared or divided so that their work load is commensurate with their new hours?
- Will additional staff be required to fill in for participating employees?
- How will backfill staff be selected?

These issues must be resolved on a case-by-case basis. The proposal should suggest a workable mechanism (usually a job redefinition committee) that will ensure that these issues are decided fairly. Sample language might read:

> The employee, the employee's immediate supervisor and a designated representative of the personnel department would consitute a committee to redesign the participant's job description in a way that is commensurate with the employee's new hours. If new staff will be hired to fill in for the participating employee, this committee would also be responsible for approving the appointment.
>
> The committee would produce a written plan which must be approved by both the head of the department concerned and that department's union steward. The department head would be in charge of ensuring that the plan will enable the company to meet its normal operational goals. The union steward would be responsible for ensuring that the plan does not place unfair demands on either the participating employee or the employee's co-workers.
>
> Where possible, backfill employees would be hired from the recall list on a seniority basis. If the backfill arrangement involves a significant sharing of duties, the compatibility of the regular and backfill employees would supercede seniority as a hiring criteria.

4. Time schedules

Describe the kinds of work schedules that are possible under the program, noting any legal restrictions. Describe appropriate mechanisms for determining individual schedules. (This is usually the task of a job redefinition committee.) Mention any provisions for overlapping schedules or trading hours and any special arrangements for staff meetings, in-service training, vacation time and statutory holidays.

5. Continuity/communication concerns

How will the new work arrangement affect office procedures and patterns of staff communication? Describe any general rules, for example: "Staff meetings will be attended by the job sharer who is on duty at the time. That person will be responsible for communicating the results of the meeting to the off-duty partner."

Describe mechanisms for maintaining continuity in an explanatory paragraph: "All job sharers will be expected to complete tasks and return files before the end of their shift. If necessary, partners will use a change-over file to transfer information."

In programs where communication/continuity patterns are expected to be a major problem (job sharing, phased retirement), it may be useful to make this issue part of the responsibility of the job redefinition committee: "The job redefinition committee will try to foresee potential communication/continuity problems and suggest mechanisms to avoid or overcome these problems."

Mechanisms may be needed to deal with communication/continuity in the following areas:

- staff meeting/staff memos.
- schedule postings.
- urgent calls or crisis situations.
- front-line coverage/on-call functions.
- unfinished tasks and follow-up.
- continuity with clients.
- information exchange between regular and backfill staff.
- in-service training programs.

6. Suggested benefit package

Flexitime, telecommuting, compressed work weeks and banked overtime have no effect on benefit packages because they involve the standard number of working hours. However, anyone proposing a compressed work week must specify a mechanism for dealing with statutory holidays.

People who want short-term leave (less than 90 days), paid leave, phased retirement or cuts in work time of 10 per cent or less can ask for full fringe benefits. Older workers should also deal with the question of pension plan contributions: for example, "Contributions to the pension plan will continue at the normal rate for full-time employment."

For options not mentioned above, the best strategy is to ask for a benefit package that is prorated according to the number of hours worked. Prorated benefits add to the persuasiveness of your proposal because they have little or no effect on an employer's payroll costs. At the same time, employees who get prorated benefits have a better deal than most casual part-time staff. (See also "The Politics of Benefits," page 110.)

In this section, you need to list all your present benefits and indicate how they will be affected by your proposal. It also helps to introduce this section with a short statement of principle: "Fringe benefits are part of an employee's total wage package, and any employee on reduced hours deserves an approximately proportionate share of benefits or a cash payment in lieu of partial benefits."

The method of prorating benefits depends on whether your employer uses a "cafeteria-style" benefit plan or a "fixed-menu" approach. In a fixed-menu system, everyone gets a standard benefit package; in the cafeteria-style approach, new employees are allowed to build their own benefit package from a range of choices.

If your organization has a cafeteria-style system, the proposal should state that participants will be able to tailor their benefit packages to suit individual needs: "In consultation with the job redefinition committee, participants will select their own benefit package, the cost of which cannot exceed an hours-based proration of the normal full-time allowance."

If your organization has a standard benefit plan, benefits for all participants in the work option program will need to be prorated in the same way. In that case, the proposal should suggest a standard formula for proration. It is sometimes useful to survey potential participants to find out which benefits they want to keep in full, which benefits they are willing to have prorated and which benefits they can do without (or pay for privately).

The easiest way to organize this section is to list all current benefits and describe how they would change under the program.

- *Unemployment Insurance, Canada Pension Plan and Worker's Compensation*

UIC, CPP (or QPP) and Worker's Compensation contributions are all based on a percentage of income. In your proposal, you can simply say, "UIC, CPP and Worker's Compensation prorate automatically when income is reduced."

- *Vacation and sick leave*

Vacation and sick leave will normally be "prorated as a proportion of the normal full-time allotment."

- *Statutory holidays*

Statutory holidays can be prorated—although sometimes with difficulty. If you are proposing a shorter work day, "statutory holidays prorate automatically." If you are proposing a shorter work year, there would normally be "no payment for statutory holidays that fall during time off."

If you are proposing a shorter work week, the mechanics of prorating statutory holidays can be extremely complicated. The simplest method is to say that "If a statutory holiday falls on a scheduled work day, the employee will receive payment for the number of hours the employee would be expected to work." Employees who work most Mondays will come out ahead by this arrangement; employees who don't work Mondays will be somewhat penalized. (Job sharers often trade schedules in order to apportion statutory holidays fairly.)

The other alternative is to say that "All statutory holidays will be prorated." In that case, an employee who works three-quarters time would get three-quarters of a day's pay for each statutory holiday whether the employee was scheduled to work that day or not. This approach is fairer, but it tends to cause fluctuations in paycheques. They are smaller when a statutory holiday falls on a scheduled work day and larger if it falls on a day when you are not scheduled to work. Sometimes, employees arrange to adjust their work hours in weeks that contain a statutory holiday in order to equalize their paycheques.

The following items refer to supplementary benefits. Unlike the previous statutory benefits, most supplementary benefits are difficult, if not impossible, to prorate. The usual solution is to alter the whole package of supplementary benefits in a way that reduces the cost by the same percentage as the reduction in work hours. For example, if work hours are reduced by 25 per cent, the overall cost of supplementary benefits should be reduced by one-quarter. Try to retain the most important benefits or those that would be more expensive if purchased privately.

If you ask your union or the personnel department for the exact cost of each supplementary benefit, you will be able to divide the package fairly accurately; otherwise you will have to make a rough estimate and negotiate the final details later.

- *Registered Retirement Savings Plans*

RRSPs can be purchased privately for about the same price.

- *Company pension plans*

Company pension plans vary greatly in their structure and the basis for calculating pension income. Some pension plans are administered by the employer, and others are administered by an outside pension fund. Changing the rules is a lot harder in the latter case.

Some plans base pensions on lifetime earnings; in that case, working less for a few years has a relatively small effect, even if those years are the final years of employment. In some plans, earnings in the last five years of employment have a big effect on pension income, regardless of years of service. In that case, most employees won't be able to afford to work less prior to retirement without a change in the pension plan.

Some plans base pensions on the level of contributions to the plan. In that case, reduced work hours have absolutely no effect on pension as long as the employee and/or the employer continue to make contributions as though the employee were working full-time.

Some plans will disqualify employees who work less than full-time. Others allow employees to prorate their years of service: for example, every year of half-time work is equivalent to six months of full-time service.

Ask your union steward or the personnel office for information about the pension plan and the effect of reduced work hours. If you can't find out what the options are (or you don't understand them), it is often wise to say, "This proposal is contingent on arrangements for pension contributions that will not adversely affect participants' future pensions."

- *Provincial medical insurance premiums*

Provincial medical insurance premiums can be dealt with in a number of ways. Because participants can buy their own coverage directly from the province, this is a reasonable benefit to trade for a full benefit elsewhere. All or part of the cost of medical insurance premiums can be covered by a payroll deduction. Coverage can be prorated from "family" to "self." Full coverage can be retained by waiving other benefits.

- *Dental insurance plans and extended medical insurance*

These are expensive to buy privately, so these benefits should be retained in full if possible, either by waiving other benefits or by increasing the employee's share of premiums through payroll deductions.

- *Group life, disability insurance and short-term illness insurance plans*

These are normally based on a percentage of salary, so they "prorate automatically according to income." Some plans have rules excluding part-time employees. In other plans the rules allow participants to continue contributing as if they were working full-time.

- *Profit-sharing plans*

Profit-sharing dividends are usually received as a percentage of income, so they also "prorate automatically."

- *Other benefits*

Other benefits may include stock options, health club memberships, Employee Assistance Plan services. etc. These are unusual, and although they may be valuable to employees, they are often hard to evaluate in hard figures. Don't bother trying to set a price on them, and don't mention them in your proposal.

If you are tearing your hair trying to work out a fair proration of benefits, don't worry. That's only normal. Do the best you can and go on to the next step. The personnel department will have to handle anything you can't deal with. That's their job, after all.

7. Costs

Employers often fear that nonstandard work schedules will cost them money. Itemizing costs and potential savings usually makes it clear that the expense involved is manageable. The following costs are worth considering.

- If your proposal involves adding additional part-time positions, the cost in paperwork will be approximately $100 per year for each additional employee.
- If you are asking to retain full benefits, itemize the benefits and, if possible, indicate the cost. (The personnel manager and your union financial agent should both have this information.)

- When positions with a salary significantly over $25,000 per year are reduced in hours and backfilled, it results in "a slight increase in employer UIC, CPP and Worker's Compensation payments due to the effect of contribution ceilings." (No extra cost is incurred if the salary is $25,000 or under.)
- If your proposal requires extra office space, staff training, extra staff meetings or overlap time, list them as costs with an estimated dollar value, if possible.
- List any rental expenses (special equipment, etc.).

The following areas are sources of possible savings.

- If your proposal involves hiring less experienced employees as backfill staff, total wage costs may be less. (This situation occurs most frequently in phased retirement programs.)
- Using part-time employees may mean that your employer has to pay less overtime. If you know how much overtime an average full-time staff person works, you can often attach a dollar value to these savings.
- If your organization already has part-time staff, and keeps records on absenteeism, you can often make a dollar estimate of cost savings resulting from reduced absenteeism.

Your proposal should take account of the following start-up costs:

- the cost of hiring and training backfill staff.
- the cost of purchasing extra equipment.
- the time personnel department staff will spend designing and implementing the program.

Try to collect enough hard numbers to make a clear statement such as: "This job sharing arrangement will have an estimated net cost of $300 per year for every job affected, primarily in increased benefit costs." It's also a good idea to mention aspects of the proposal that will avoid additional costs: "Because the organization has a large pool of former employees who can be recruited as backfill staff, training costs will be minimal."

8. Advantages and disadvantages

List all the possible advantages and disadvantages that the work option program will create for your employer. Mention any concerns that you have dealt with in the design of the program: "Some modified work week programs have experienced difficulties with Monday and Friday coverage, but allocating days off by means of a rota system will ensure equal coverage throughout the week." Refer to any valid "test" situation relevant to an advantage or a possible concern: for example, "One potential concern relates to the possibility that part-time operating room nurses might get out of practice in dealing with emergency procedures. However, this problem has not developed in situations where nurses employed on a casual basis work a similar number of shifts."

Possible advantages include:

- reduced absenteeism.
- reduced staff turnover.
- improved morale.
- increased productivity.
- better peak coverage.
- extended hours coverage.
- lunch hour/holiday/vacation coverage.
- emergency/overtime coverage.
- extra skills/specialized skills.
- health and safety benefits.
- cost savings.

Possible problem areas include:

- continuity.
- communication.
- staff meetings/staff training.
- supervision.
- uneven skill levels.
- co-worker attitudes.
- scheduling confusion.
- extra costs.

Try to be even handed in assessing advantages and disadvantages. Work options should not be presented as a panacea, but rather as a workable trade-off in which the advantages outweigh the problems. (Note: in some proposals, "Advantages and disadvantages," called "Rationale," will fit best immediately after the Introduction.)

9. Local examples

Your case will be stronger if you can mention other employers (or individual "exceptions" in your own organization) who have had success with the system you are proposing. It helps if you can find examples which are a) fairly local b) in the same occupational area and c) in the same industry. For example, policemen who want to work permanent part-time should make a point of mentioning the fact that the police officers in a nearby community are already working permanent part-time (particularly if the police chief thinks the program is a success).

Question professional acquaintances and your union; make a few discreet calls to the personnel departments of other organizations. You may be able to uncover an example that will strengthen your case and perhaps give you some good ideas to use in the design of your own proposal.

10. A plan for implementation

A plan for implementation should include:

- a suggested starting date.
- a suggested trial period.
- suggested procedures for finalizing details of the new arrangement.

A suggested starting date reminds management about the need to make a decision. A trial period protects both you and your employer; it allows both parties to test the arrangement without making an irrevocable decision. Many programs also limit the trial period to a certain number of participants. This also helps allay the fears of management.

A suggested framework for a method of reaching a final agreement is extremely important. The structure should allow a reasonable amount of consultation. A committee made up of a union representative, a representative of the personnel department, a management representative and someone who represents prospective participants in the program can provide a forum for negotiation, compromise and resolution of the irksome details that inevitably arise. This committee can also be recalled on an as-needed basis to deal with problems, changes or expansion of the program.

The final agreement should be a written document. This document often takes the form of a memorandum of agreement between the employer and the union which states that the program is a temporary ex-

periment which must be evaluated before the next contract talks. It includes the understanding that terms for continuing the program would be
part of the collective agreement.

In an initial proposal, it isn't necessary to go into a lot of detail about
how the program will be implemented; much of that can be worked out in
committee. However, any essential aspects of the implementation procedure should be spelled out: for example, "The phased retirement program
will not begin until necessary changes in the pension agreement have been
made and approved by an outside legal authority."

Features of the program which would facilitate the implementation
process should also be mentioned: for example, "To minimize misunder-
standings, participants in the V-Time program should receive an orientation package that describes the effect of the program on their wages,
benefits, seniority and duty assignments."

For a more concrete idea of what a collective work option proposal
involves, take a look at the sample proposal starting on the next page.

Proposal for a Three-Quarter Time Program

Introduction

This is a proposal for an expanded permanent part-time program for the nursing staff in the emergency operating room (EOR) unit of the King William Hospital. The proposed program would be built around a rotation whereby four staff would split three current full-time positions.

Eligibility Criteria/Participants

Initially the program would involve three members of the current full-time staff (Sylvia Bains, Joanne Hopkirk, and Carol Casey) plus a former staff member (Marie Chasse) rehired on a contract basis. If the three-quarter time option proves successful we hope the hospital will offer the same arrangement to other trios of nurses who request it.

Backfill Staffing/Job Redefinition

When the three current staff cut back to three-quarter time, one additional three-quarter time nurse will be needed to cover the shortfall in hours. Marie is trained in EOR procedures and has a good work record. Duties and responsibilities would be the same as for full-time nurses.

Schedules

Four part-time nurses will split three full-time rotations. Instead of working 32 12-hour shifts in a 10-week period, each part-time nurse would work 24 12-hour shifts every 10 weeks. To show how the schedule would work in practice, we have drawn up a sample duty roster for a three-week period in January.

Under the current arrangement the schedule for these three weeks would be (see overleaf):

Day of Month	0 1	0 2	0 3	0 4	0 5	0 6	0 7	0 8	0 9	1 0	1 1	1 2	1 3	1 4	1 5	1 6	1 7	1 8	1 9	2 0	2 1
Sylvia		D	D	N	N						D	D	N	N						D	D
Joanne	N	N					D	D	N	N						D	D	N	N		
Carol	D	D	N					D	D	N	N							D	D	N	N

(D = Day Shift, N = Night Shift)

Under the proposed arrangement the schedule for the same period would be:

Day of Month	0 1	0 2	0 3	0 4	0 5	0 6	0 7	0 8	0 9	1 0	1 1	1 2	1 3	1 4	1 5	1 6	1 7	1 8	1 9	2 0	2 1
Sylvia			D	N	N							D	N	N							D
Joanne	N	N					D	N	N							D	N	N			
Carol	D	D	N						D	N	N							D	N	N	
Marie		D					D		D		D					D		D		D	

This schedule was designed to fit Marie's preference for working days only. The schedule would be different under other circumstances.

Communication/Continuity Concerns

The new arrangement should not affect continuity of patient care because patients are rarely on the EOR unit for more than 24 hours.

Existing communication systems and procedures could easily accommodate the new arrangement. (All hospital communication systems are designed to be able to accommodate a complete changeover of staff every 12 hours.) The new schedules will be somewhat more irregular than the standard full-time shift rotation. However, any member of staff can consult the monthly register to find out which nurses will be working at a particular time.

Suggested Benefit Package

UIC, CPP, Worker's Compensation, pension benefits and long-term disability insurance would all be prorated automatically because contributions and benefits would be based on a percentage of wages.

Sick leave, vacation, maternity leave and holidays would all be prorated according to the formula for part-time staff contained in the collective agreement.

Page 2

According to provisions for part-time staff contained in the existing collective agreement, the hospital would continue to pay full medical, dental, extended medical, and group life insurance premiums.

For purposes of accumulating service increments, pension credits and seniority, every 1875 hours worked would be considered equivalent to one year of service, as per the terms of the existing collective agreement.

Cost Analysis

Employer contributions to UIC, CPP, Worker's Compensation, the pension plan and long-term disability insurance all prorate automatically. No extra costs would be involved.

Vacation, holiday pay and maternity leave all prorate automatically. No extra costs would be involved.

For every three full-time positions, the hospital would have to fund four sets of supplementary benefits packages. This would amount to approximately $82 per month or $1000 per year (medical plan = $20/month; dental plan = $40/month; group life = $7/month; extended medical = $15/month).

Labour Canada estimates the cost in paperwork of adding one more person to the payroll at approximately $100/year.

The cost of in-service training for one extra staff member is difficult to estimate, but would probably not be more than $100 per year.

The hospital will save money on sick leave benefits because part-time staff use less sick leave than full-time staff. Over the past year, full-time staff took an average of 100 hours of sick leave, but part-time staff took an average of only 85 hours of sick leave per full-time equivalent (FTE). If the four part-time staff on this program use 45 hours less sick leave per year (100 - 85 x 3 = 45), the hospital will save $700/year (45 hours x $16/hour = $700).

The hospital will save money on overtime pay because three-quarter time staff would usually work extra hours at straight-time pay. Last year, full-time staff worked an average of 70 hours of overtime at time-and-a-half rates. If the four part-time staff work a total of 150 extra hours at straight-time rates, the hospital would save $1200 per year (150 hours x $8 premium for overtime = $1200).

Page 3

Total additional costs under the new arrangement would be more than offset by estimated savings. Costs would equal $1200 for three FTEs or $400 per FTE. Estimated savings would equal $1900 for three FTEs or $600 per FTE. Despite higher benefit costs, overall personnel costs would be less.

Advantages

REDUCED STRESS: Nursing is physically and emotionally demanding. Although the 12-hour shifts allow longer periods of time off, they also cause more fatigue, particularly among older nurses and those with family responsibilities. EOR positions are particularly stressful. The work load is unpredictable, and patients are often severely injured. In many cases, the work requires quick thinking and a high level of concentration; there is little or no room for error.

REDUCED TURNOVER AND EASIER RECRUITMENT: More than half of the nurses on the EOR unit say they plan to leave within the next two or three years if they can't find a way to lighten their work load. Most of these nurses say they would stay if they were offered positions at three-quarter time. Several nurses who have left the unit for health or family reasons say they would be willing to return to a three-quarter time schedule. As well as reducing turnover, the three-quarter time option would be a powerful recruiting tool. Lower rates of turnover and absenteeism would mean fewer trainee and casual staff on the unit. This is an important consideration on a unit where quick and accurate response to a crisis is essential.

EMERGENCY BACK-UP: The use of three-quarter time staff would also provide a trained reserve in the event of a major medical disaster.

The drawbacks of the program would be minor. Some additional support services might be required for a somewhat larger staff. The work schedules of nurses on three-quarter time would also be somewhat less regular and predictable.

Local Examples

Many B.C. hospitals use three-quarter time positions for peak coverage, with no apparent problems reported. Split rotations are also not unusual; for example, the Pearkes Clinic of the Queen Alexandra

Page 4

Hospital employs five health care workers who split 3.5 positions in a manner very similar to that described in this proposal, and the arrangement has proved satisfactory for all concerned.

Implementation

We would suggest that the new arrangement be given a trial period of three rotation cycles (a total of 30 weeks) starting January 1st.

If the program were cancelled at the end of the trial period, the contract for the person rehired would not be renewed. The new arrangement requires no changes to the collective agreement. We recommend that all parties sign a trial agreement that outlines the terms of the arrangement, its effect on scheduling and benefits, and contingency plans.

We also recommend that the supervisor in charge of scheduling shifts coordinate the evaluation of the trial program. In addition to collecting feedback from the participating nurses and their supervisors, she would also be asked to tabulate absenteeism and overtime use for the purpose of making a proper cost analysis.

Step Seven

Putting Work In Its Place

 Expediting the Approval Process

Tactics are important in getting a work option proposal approved. In a large organization, the approval process may take anywhere from six to 18 months, but careful tactics can sometimes speed the process.

With individual proposals, the first question is where to send your proposal. In most cases, you should give it to your immediate supervisor. However, if you know that your immediate supervisor is adamantly opposed to the idea, you could send your proposal to someone higher up in the administration instead. This is a risky strategy, but it has worked on occasion.

If a union is involved, someone from the union should get a copy; if you know of someone in the union leadership who has been supportive or responsive to your needs in the past, send a copy to that person. If the personnel department is likely to be supportive, send them a copy. You want to be sure that any possible allies know about your proposal and have a reason for interceding on your behalf.

Make up a short covering letter to go with each copy of the proposal you send out: that will make it seem less formal. It also gives you a chance to say why that person is being sent a copy and what action you expect.

Group or union proposals usually go to the head of the personnel department and someone fairly high up in management. Again, prospective allies should always receive a copy of the proposal. It isn't always necessary to inform people who are likely to oppose the idea.

It is not a good idea to introduce work option proposals in contract bargaining talks. In most cases, work options start as temporary experiments under a memorandum of agreement between the union and management. However, the collective agreement may contain a clause to the effect that "Work scheduling experiments may be conducted from time to time during the life of this contract by mutual agreement between the union and the employer."

There are at least three reasons why contract talks are not a good way to initiate work option programs.

- The atmosphere in contract talks is often adversarial.
- It takes more time to set up a good option program than is available during contract talks.

- Most option programs need time to settle in. Until a program is running smoothly, it shouldn't be "cast in stone" by including it in the collective agreement.

After an option program has had a couple of years to mature and develop, both sides are often willing to make it a part of the collective agreement without argument.

Once you have submitted your proposal, you have to be diplomatic about pushing for approval. Without some urging from you or someone who is backing you, your proposal could get stuck in the pipe. On the other hand, too much pushing will arouse antagonism. A successful strategy usually takes one of two approaches: curiosity ("I had hoped to hear something about my proposal by now. Can you tell me what's holding it up?") or helpful concern ("I understand that my proposal has gone to you for consideration. If you have any questions, I would be happy to answer them.").

Sometimes, management will try to discourage you by stalling on a decision. If that happens, pressure from your union may be necessary.

Your employer may make a counter proposal. Think about what compromise arrangement you would be willing to accept and what kind of counter-proposal you could make.

You should also consider what you would do if your employer refuses to negotiate. Will you quietly begin looking for another job? Will you quit outright? Will you raise the issue with your union? Will you look at self-employment or going back to school?

If you are convinced that you have other options, you can often press your case more vigorously. Sometimes management will say "yes" simply because it becomes harder and harder to keep saying "no." The process of shepherding a proposal through to approval almost always requires patience, tenacity and nerve, particularly in a large organization.

A final note to those who are worried about losing their job because of a request for flexible hours. A proposal to change your hours is not a refusal to fulfill your contract. A proposal simply says, "If we can both agree, I would like to change my work schedule." If your employer were to fire you for submitting a proposal, you could sue for wrongful dismissal, and you would probably win.

···IT'S A NOTE FROM FARMER JONES ··· HE AGREES TO ALL OUR DEMANDS EXCEPT MATERNITY LEAVE FOR THE HENS···

Implementing Your Program

Your proposal should include a basic plan for implementation. Once your proposal is approved, all you have to do is make sure you cover all the steps in your plan. Implementing an individual program usually involves little more than drawing up a written agreement and getting it signed. Be sure to read the paragraph below on written agreements for a checklist of what to include.

In group programs, implementation will involve some or all of the following items. (For multiple option programs, see also "The Flexible Workplace," page 248.)

NEEDS SURVEY

A needs survey will determine how many employees are interested in the program and how they would prefer to arrange their hours. Before arranging relief coverage for a banked overtime, flexitime or V-Time system, you need some idea of the expected pattern of use. A needs survey is usually a short, anonymous questionnaire which provides rough estimates for use in the planning process.

HOURS OF WORK COMMITTEE

An hours of work committee serves several purposes. It can draft a final agreement, produce policy and briefing documents, screen applications, settle disputes, monitor results and co-ordinate housekeeping tasks.

WRITTEN AGREEMENT

A written agreement ensures that both sides have the same understanding of the rules. The written agreement should contain the following clauses.

- Describe clearly any changes in your benefit package, especially your pension.
- Describe any effects on your seniority, job classification and salary.
- List any changes in your duties or responsibilities.

- Describe specific features of your new schedule, including any agreements about statutory holidays, vacation time or time-trading provisions.
- Define the conditions under which you would be entitled to overtime pay.
- Specify a trial period and a starting date.
- Describe what will happen if the program is cancelled and the circumstances which would justify cancelling the program before the end of the trial period.

LEGAL REVIEW

Before signing any agreement, ask the Labour Standards Branch of your provincial Ministry of Labour to confirm that it satisfies all their requirements.

APPLICATION PROCESS

The application process needs eligibility criteria, an application form and a procedure for approving applications. The process should include procedures for job redefinition, relief coverage, changes to the benefit package and so on. Every successful applicant to the program should have an individualized written agreement similar to the document described above.

BRIEFING MATERIALS/POLICY STATEMENTS

All those directly or indirectly affected by the new program should receive advance notice of the changes and a basic orientation in the operation of the new system. Any policy changes (for example, changes in overtime policy) should be clearly defined. Participants should have the name of a contact person who can answer questions or deal with problems. Supervisors should also be briefed on the program so that their expectations are realistic.

COMMUNICATION MECHANISMS

What changes in the filing system and office procedures will be required to accommodate the new system? How will staff meetings be scheduled? For messages, will there be a special communications log, an overlap period or a tape recorder? Is a scheduling calendar needed and if so, who needs to receive a copy?

RECORDING SYSTEMS/PAPERWORK MECHANICS

How will hours be recorded under the new system? Will changes in the mechanics of the payroll structure be needed? What changes are required in the pension plan, insurance policies or the after-hours answering service? Do signs listing office hours need to be updated?

EQUIPMENT

Are any special equipment purchases required? Who will be responsible for purchasing equipment? Are extra keys, uniforms, desks or computers needed? Does the phone or switchboard system need changing?

BACKFILL STAFFING

Who will hire backfill staff? How will they be recruited? What method will be used to schedule backfill staff? Who will be responsible for scheduling? How much training will the new staff need? Who will be responsible for training?

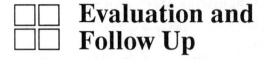 Evaluation and Follow Up

Work option programs are rarely problem free, and "bugs" usually show up within the first year. It is almost impossible to foresee all the circumstances that could affect the smooth running of your plan. Time and effort spent evaluating and adjusting your program during the trial period can often spell the difference between wholehearted support by your employer and reluctant acceptance.

It is useful to solicit early feedback from your co-workers, clients and supervisor. By asking "Has my new schedule caused you any problems?" you may uncover minor problems and resentments before they escalate into major issues. If you ask, "Is there any way we could avoid this problem in the future?" you may be able to involve the other person in the process of finding ways to make the program more effective. People who feel consulted and included are far less likely to attack your program when it is being evaluated.

Minor changes in office procedures can often enhance the advantages of the new schedule and minimize the difficulties. Your program doesn't have to be problem free at evaluation time, as long as it appears to have more advantages than drawbacks.

During the trial period, you can monitor "vital signs" and collect a mental file of positive comments. Look for information that can be useful at evaluation time. Is absenteeism down measurably? Have fewer customer complaints been recorded? Have there been fewer delays in processing orders?

It's also important to be aware of your own reactions during the trial period. Sometimes the results of a change in hours are unexpected: the reality of the new schedule may not live up to your expectations. The end of the trial period is a natural time to ask for changes which would make the program work better for you or to cancel the program if that's your decision.

Communication patterns usually require some adjustment in order to get the best results. Sometimes the problems involve feelings rather than the actual exchange of information. If someone (you, a co-worker or your supervisor) feels out of touch or as though they have lost control of the situation, the strain may have less to do with the efficiency of the system than with the friendships in the work place or the power relationships between people. Sometimes going out for lunch or having a beer together after work will improve the personal relationships that are also a part of the work place. This area is particularly important for job sharing partners.

Programs designed for a single individual do not require an elaborate process of evaluation. A one-page survey for co-workers and selected clients (if that's appropriate) can produce useful feedback. The kind of questions to ask include:

- How has the new arrangement affected you?
- What problems have you found with the new arrangement?
- Are these problems manageable? How could they be minimized?
- What benefits do you see in the new arrangement?
- Do you see any reason why the new arrangement should not continue?
- Do you have any other comments or suggestions?

You and your supervisor should also answer the survey in order to establish a basis for your discussion. Collect any available data on absenteeism, productivity changes, overtime use, etc.

You and your supervisor may be the only people who need to be involved in the formal evaluation. However, if you suspect that your supervisor wants to cancel the program, you may want to ask for a representative of the personnel department to be present at the meeting with your supervisor. It can be useful to have an objective third party lead the discussion in any case.

The result of the evaluation meeting should be a report which summarizes the findings and makes one of three recommendations.

1. The program should be continued on an ongoing basis.
2. The program should be changed and a second trial period instituted.
3. The program should be cancelled.

The evaluation report may be written by anyone who was present at the evaluation meeting, but it should be ratified by everyone involved before it is submitted to upper management.

Most work option programs pass evaluation easily. In fact, after a year or so, other people tend to forget that you ever worked any other way.

A more elaborate evaluation procedure is necessary when work option programs involve several people, especially if they are serving as a pilot for larger programs. One person is usually delegated to study the program and prepare a report. The report then forms the basis for discussions in the hours of work committee, which makes recommendations as to the future of the program.

The report writer is usually a member of the hours of work committee, but the writer may also be a representative of the personnel department. Outside consultants may also be used. In addition to administering written questionnaires to participants, their co-workers and their supervisors, the report writer may also conduct telephone or face-to-face interviews.

A more objective assessment of the program can be achieved if control data can be obtained (either "before" data or data from a comparable unit still on traditional schedules). One of the problems in analyzing the effect of work option programs on productivity is that perceptions are often colored by subjective attitudes and feelings about the program. The review process will also seem more positive if both the report writer and the hours of work committee approach the evaluation from the standpoint of "How can the program be made most effective?" rather than "Should the program be continued?"

When the hours of work committee has accepted the report and made any necessary additions, changes and/or recommendations, the report should be submitted to management and the union executive for further action or comment. It is also advisable to circulate copies of the final report to those who participated in the evaluation.

When a work option program is to be expanded from the pilot stage to a full-scale program, it is often wise to phase in changes in order to minimize confusion and continuity problems while the new system is settling in. An exception to this rule involves compressed work weeks, where a mixture of old and new schedules may be more problematic than changing everyone's schedule at once. Once a program has final approval, it should be included in both the collective agreement and the personnel policy manual. This establishes the program as an integral part of the organization's operation.

Special
Cases/
Further
Resources

Work Options as an Alternative to Layoffs

Layoffs are usually preceded by rumors, hints and official warnings. Instead of waiting passively for the axe to fall, employees at many Canadian work places have used this time to explore work options as a way of avoiding impending layoffs. In most work places, some people would welcome the opportunity to work less than full-time. By allowing these employees to reduce their hours, work options can make more work available for others. At one time or another, job sharing, leave programs, V-Time, banked overtime and retirement options have all been used to reduce or eliminate the threat of layoffs.

Employers know that layoffs are bad for morale and that concern about job security has a negative effect on productivity. Though this atmosphere is bad in every other way, it can be a good opportunity for introducing the idea of a work option program. Employers and unions who wouldn't normally agree to innovations in work schedules will often listen when it's clear that changes could save jobs. If you have been turned down before, this is a good time to try again.

When work options are being considered as an alternative to layoffs, as many people as possible should be involved in the discussions. In this situation, signs of strong support on the shop floor will often influence the decision of management.

Start by forming an organizing committee made up of people who have some interest in the concept. Circulate a memo about the formation of the committee. This will serve two purposes: it will strengthen awareness of the threat of layoffs and enable supporters to find you. Don't assume that management or the union will take the initiative in suggesting work options as a solution for layoffs. In most cases, the initiative has come from an informal group of employees.

The various work options are not all equally effective at avoiding layoffs. Job sharing usually appeals to five or 10 percent of employees, but it would preserve only half as many jobs. More people are likely to participate if the work force is largely female or if it contains a large number of older workers. Programs that allow smaller cuts in work time (V-Time or permanent part-time) appeal to more people and may increase job opportunities by as much as 10 per cent.

Leave programs (either deferred salary arrangements or unpaid educational leave) typically appeal to about five per cent of the work force. Twenty-five to 50 per cent of workers over 55 will be interested in phased retirement programs or opportunities for early retirement with a bridging pension. (This often constitutes a legitimate use of the surplus that many pension funds now contain.)

If compulsory banked overtime is used to convert overtime hours and premium rates into full-time equivalents, the number of jobs created will depend on the average amount of overtime in your work place. Because men are usually less interested than women in reducing their hours of work, compulsory banked overtime may be the least painful and most effective way to reduce staff levels when the work force is predominantly male. This alternative is less attractive than voluntary work options, but it is obviously preferable to layoffs.

Programs that combine more than one work option can increase the savings in "full-time equivalents" (FTEs). Job sharing, short-term leaves, phased retirement and permanent part-time can all be offered under the general umbrella of V-Time. For this reason, V-Time is usually the preferred multiple-option approach. (V-Time and banked overtime can fit together neatly if one relief staff can be used for both.)

When you are first thinking about work options as an alternative to layoffs, a needs survey can help determine which options should be offered. In addition to explaining the way different options work, the survey should mention any safeguards and protections to be included in the program.

Safeguards can help to encourage maximum participation. Voluntary programs should be free of any real or perceived compulsory features, and seniority should be based on a calendar system so that employees who reduce their hours will not lose their place on the seniority list. An automatic right to return to full-time after six months or a year is another reassuring feature. Older workers are unlikely to participate unless the pension plan is altered to protect their retirement income. Maintaining full benefits for those who make small cuts in work time is an added incentive to participation.

If the number of planned layoffs is large (20 per cent or more), voluntary work options may not have enough impact to avoid layoffs. In these circumstances, work sharing may be a better alternative, particularly if the layoffs are temporary. Work sharing involves an across-the-board reduction in work hours. The typical solution is a four-day week, although cuts sometimes go deeper.

Compulsory reductions in work hours always cause emotional and economic trauma, but a sense of solidarity can develop when everyone faces the same reductions. And working less doesn't damage a person's self-respect as much as unemployment does. Sometimes, the extra free time is welcome despite the loss of income. Work sharing is never entirely voluntary, because it only occurs in the shadow of impending layoffs; however, it usually occurs because everyone has accepted the necessity to work less in order to avoid layoffs for some.

When all employees agree to reduce their hours equally in order to avoid temporary layoffs, they become eligible for a federal program called Work Sharing, which allows them to collect unemployment insurance for the days they don't work. Under this program, employees on a four-day week would take home about 92 per cent of their full-time income. Employees on a three-day week would take home approximately 84 per cent of their usual income. An employee who is eventually laid off becomes eligible for full unemployment insurance with only a small penalty.

The work sharing program has a number of eligibility rules. All employees in a given unit must participate voluntarily; in an organized work place, the union must approve the program, and the reduction in work hours must be temporary. For more information, contact your local Canada Employment Centre.

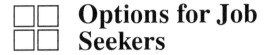 # Options for Job Seekers

Everything we have said so far has been directed towards working people who want to reduce or rearrange their hours. What if you are unemployed and want a part-time job or one that offers flexible hours? It isn't easy to go looking for an alternative work arrangement, but it's not impossible either. Job seekers have had success with the following strategies.

JOINT JOB SEARCH

If you are sure that you don't want full-time work, you have nothing to lose by locating a compatible partner and looking for work as a job sharing pair. Sometimes this will put you at a disadvantage compared to other candidates, but not always. Occasionally, an employer will favor a pair of applicants over an individual. In one case, for example, a shipper-receiver position went to two sisters because the arrangement gave the employer the capacity for double coverage on heavy days. In another case, a teaching position went to two teachers who jointly offered a range of specialties rarely available in a single teacher.

To be successful at joint job search, you must do much of the "partnering" work in advance. First, find a partner with whom you feel comfortable, preferably someone with whom you have worked in the past and whom you know well. Figure out your preferred schedules and the mechanisms you intend to use to exchange information. Talk to each other about the way you like to organize things, your philosophy of work, your work history, your likes and dislikes on the job, etc. This will make you a functioning team by the time you get to a job interview.

If you plan to split your hours unequally, look closely at how you would divide the work and how you would share authority. Discuss in advance the extent to which you are willing to cover for each other for vacations or illness and whether you are willing to work overtime to cover peak periods. These can be important selling points for an employer — but don't promise anything you are not able to deliver.

Your job search will help develop the teamwork necessary for a good partnership. Two people's ideas, energy and enthusiasm can make the process of finding a job easier. Looking for a job together is also an excellent opportunity to learn how to support one another.

Joint job search involves developing a team presentation. List your qualifications and your work histories side by side in a joint resume. Mention briefly how you would work as a team and the advantages of a team approach. Have a friend pretend to be an employer and practice operating as a team in the job interview situation. Make sure you are well informed about job sharing so that you can answer employers' questions.

FIND A PARTNER WHO HAS A JOB

Talk to your friends, professional associates and employees at your former places of employment. Who feels overloaded and wants to cut back? Lend this book to friends who are employed. Don't feel embarrassed about asking: you aren't looking for charity; you are looking for someone who has a good reason for wanting to work less. (If you want to work nearly full-time—say, four days a week—you may need to find more than one partner.)

A proposal for a change in work scheduling should come from the working partner, but there's no reason why you shouldn't do most of the work involved in writing and designing the proposal. Since you are unemployed, you have more free time. Just be sure that the plan you develop accurately reflects your partner's needs and wants; if not, your partner may lose interest. Prepare your resume and include it as an appendix to the proposal. The boss could accept the proposal without necessarily hiring you as a part of the package; you have to show that you are the best person for the job.

NEGOTIATE AT JOB INTERVIEWS

Even if you are not interested in a standard schedule, there is no reason why you can't apply for a full-time position and negotiate your hours during the job interview. You may discover that your preferences and the needs of your prospective employer are well matched.

NEGOTIATE AT THE POINT OF HIRING

If you are willing to work regular hours if you have to, you can wait and try negotiating when you have been offered a position. Under the right circumstances, flexitime, compressed work weeks, V-Time, partial telecommuting and banked overtime can all be negotiated at the point of hiring. Sometimes an employer will suggest that you postpone the issue until the end of your probationary period.

PAY YOUR DUES AND THEN ASK

Sometimes the only way to get the work schedule you want is to wait a year or so until you have proved yourself a dependable employee. You might get turned down anyway, so if you are worried about investing time in a situation that might turn sour, it would be wise to enquire about the prospects for a flexible work arrangement during the job interview.

FREELANCE OR WORK ON A CONTRACT BASIS

Freelance and contract staff enjoy a degree of flexibility in their work schedules that is seldom if ever accorded to regular staff. The disadvantage is that freelancers and contract workers have little or no job security.

LOOK FOR PERMANENT PART-TIME EMPLOYMENT

A growing number of employers offer good wages, benefits and job security to part-time employees. Many employers don't bother to advertise part-time jobs; instead, they hire from applications on file. By targeting the companies you would like to work for and making sure they have you listed as available for part-time work, you can tap the hidden job market for permanent part-time staff.

LOOK FOR A RELIEF STAFF POSITION

If you prefer to work part-time, if you enjoy variety and have a wide range of skills to offer, you may be able to convince an employer to hire you as a relief replacement. Large employers often recognize the fact that semi-permanent relief staff can reduce the chaos that descends whenever regular staff are on holiday. Because most employees take their vacation in the summer, this approach is best suited to people who want time off during the winter months.

Compensatory Benefit Leaves

Compensatory benefits are rights of employment. They are almost always negotiated through the collective bargaining process. There is seldom any point in approaching your employer directly about a compensatory benefit program. However, if you feel strongly that one of the benefits listed is worth fighting for, you can propose that your union include it in the next round of contract talks. Use Steps Five and Six to develop your proposal, remembering, of course, that you are trying to persuade your union instead of your employer.

Compensatory benefits include vacation time, statutory holidays, sick leave, compassionate leave, parental leave, maternity leave, paternity leave and adoption leave. For more information on your legal rights to leave, see the *Canadian Master Labour Guide* from CCH Canadian Limited, 6 Garamond Court, Don Mills, Ontario M3C 1Z5.

VACATIONS

Although Canadian employers are not legally required to give employees time off for vacation, they must provide a minimum of two weeks' vacation pay per year (equivalent to four per cent of yearly wages). Many employers offer longer paid vacations based on the number of years of service with the organization. North America has low vacation allotments compared to Europe. In France, for instance, the legal minimum is six weeks of paid vacation each year. This suggests that increased vacation time is an appropriate target for collective bargaining.

STATUTORY HOLIDAYS

Canada has nine statutory holidays per year: New Years Day, Good Friday, Victoria Day, Canada Day, Labour Day, Thanksgiving Day, Remembrance Day, Christmas Day and Boxing Day. A number of provinces designate extra statutory holidays (commonly the first Monday in August), and some collective agreements require additional paid holidays (including, in some cases, the employee's birthday). Employers are legally required to give you the day off (unpaid) to attend your own or a son or daughter's wedding.

Employers are not required to pay for a statutory holiday unless it falls on one of your normal work days, but many collective agreements have more inclusive eligibility rules. As with vacations, employers are not legally required to grant time off for statutory holidays. If you work on a holiday, however, you are entitled to receive holiday pay (at time-and-a-half) in addition to your regular daily wage.

SICK LEAVE

Sick leave usually consists of a fixed number of days off each month or year: for example, one day per month or 10 days per year. Some sick leave allowances are based on a percentage of hours worked. This system accommodates both part-time employees and those who work a lot of overtime.

In most sick leave programs, employees cannot draw against future sick leave allowances. They can claim only the amount of sick leave they have "earned" before becoming ill. Some programs allow employees to "bank" all their sick leave, and others set a maximum that can be carried over from year to year. Some programs pay for unused sick leave, and some allow unused sick leave to be rolled over into vacation time. In other programs, the rule is "what you don't use, you lose."

Sick leave is not popular with employers. It can be costly and inconvenient, and some employers are concerned about abuse of the system. Absenteeism is a serious problem that results in many more lost work days each year than strikes or work stoppages.

Unions often have to pay a high price at the bargaining table in order to negotiate a sick leave plan. Employers are often more willing to agree if the plan is designed to reward the healthy. (See "Earned Time Off," page 250.)

COMPASSIONATE LEAVE

Unpaid compassionate leave is a legal right in federal government jurisdictions and in some provinces. Many work places have some sort of compassionate leave or bereavement leave arrangement that allows employees to visit dying relatives or attend their funerals. Sometimes these arrangements are contained in the personnel guidelines or the collective agreement. At other work places there is tacit agreement that compassionate leave is granted at the discretion of the supervisor.

Usually, but not always, compassionate leave is paid leave. Sometimes compassionate leave is included within the sick leave guidelines or the personal leave guidelines. These guidelines usually define such things as eligible relatives, just cause and the length of leave allowed. Guidelines for compassionate leave should also ensure that a request can be approved quickly and easily. People in the midst of grief should not have to deal with unnecessary paperwork or delay.

Your union steward or personnel manager can tell you what compassionate leave arrangements exist at your work place. In the absence of such provisions, make a written request to your supervisor to the effect that you need time off to visit a dying relative or attend a funeral. (Depending on your supervisor and your work place, such leave may be unpaid. Be prepared for that possibility.) If your supervisor refuses on the grounds that such a request is outside his or her authority, submit your request directly to the personnel manager.

If there is an adequate sick leave program at your place of employment, perhaps the least cumbersome arrangement is to make bereavement leave a legitimate use of sick leave. This usually requires only the addition of a few clauses to the sick leave guidelines. Psychologically, modifying an existing benefit is a smaller step for management than creating a new benefit. The only drawback to this approach is the obvious one: taking time off for bereavement will cut into your illness allowance.

PARENTAL LEAVE

Although parental leave is more widespread in the U.S. and Europe than in Canada, a number of Canadian companies now have arrangements whereby parents may take time off work to care for offspring who are ill. Such arrangements are sometimes paid and sometimes unpaid.

As with bereavement leave, the immediacy of the situation may mean that you will have to apply for personal leave in order to get time off if there are no parental leave provisions at your work place. If you propose establishing a parental leave program, there are a number of possible designs you can suggest.

The most straightforward method is to incorporate a codicil into the sick leave plan allowing employees to use their own sick leave to care for sick children. (In most cases, this only legitimizes what is already happening: parents call in "sick" when their children are ill.) Again, the obvious disadvantage of this approach is that it decreases the amount of sick leave available. It is also important to consider the effect of this approach on the short-term illness insurance plan.

A second method is to have a separate paid leave allowance (similar to sick leave) on the order of a half-day a month for parental leave. This is a more cumbersome approach which requires a separate tracking arrangement. It also frequently increases employer costs and may create resentment from non parents. However, if either the employer or the union has strong pro-family values, such an arrangement will sometimes be approved.

A clause in the personnel guidelines will be enough to establish unpaid parental leave. This method is inexpensive for the employer. If an employee is willing to forego income in order to attend to the needs of a sick child, parental leave is not likely to be used frivolously. The obvious disadvantage from an employee's point of view is that most parents cannot afford many days without pay. However, if neither of the first two options are possible, unpaid parental leave at least establishes the point that parenting responsibilities are a legitimate reason to miss work.

MATERNITY LEAVE

Maternity leave is a legal right in all Canadian provinces, although the time allotted is not consistent. All provinces allow at least 17 weeks; Quebec, Saskatchewan, Alberta and B.C. allow 18 weeks. The North West Territories have no provisions for maternity leave. Women who are eligible for maternity leave can collect up to 15 weeks of unemployment insurance.

Some unions have collective agreements which require the employer to supplement unemployment insurance payments by 25 per cent (the maximum earnings allowed by Canada Employment). This increases the woman's income while on leave to 80 per cent of her regular salary. Some collective agreements also allow women to take more time off than the legal minimum (often up to six months) with a guaranteed right to return to work and the continuation of at least partial benefit coverage.

The trend today is for women to start their families later in life, have fewer children and return to work more quickly after the birth of a child. This trend has helped to control the potential costs of maternity leave provisions. It has also underlined the growing importance of the female work force in our economy and the need for employers to assist women in finding healthy ways to combine work and child rearing. Adequate maternity leave provisions are a significant part of that effort.

PATERNITY LEAVE

Unpaid paternity leave is a legal right within federal government jurisdictions and in some provinces.

Some collective agreements also allow fathers a period of leave to spend time with a newborn child. The period varies from a few days to several weeks, and the leave may be paid, partially paid or unpaid, depending on the terms of the agreement. A limited number of non-unionized work places have personnel guidelines for paternity leave. Your union steward or personnel manager should be able to tell you whether or not such provisions exist at your work place.

If there is no paternity leave where you work, you can make a proposal to institute such a program. If your need is immediate, apply for personal leave as a fall-back position.

The most straightforward way to design a paternity leave program is to model it after your firm's maternity leave provisions. In that case, you are asking for equal treatment for men and women. However, paternity leave is different from maternity leave in two important respects.

In the first place, men are not eligible for unemployment insurance during paternity leave. In the second place, conditions of eligibility for paternity leave are not clearly defined, particularly for paid leave. A woman's qualification for maternity leave is physically obvious, but paternity has some grey edges. For example, should the benefit extend to fathers who are not married (or not living with) the mother of their child?

Paternity leave programs have three important effects. First, they allow fathers time to bond with their newborn children. Second, they give fathers the opportunity to take over more of the housekeeping load while the mother is recovering from childbirth. Third, by equalizing the cost of benefits for men and women, they can help counteract unconscious prejudices against hiring women.

ADOPTION LEAVE

Unpaid adoption leave is a legal right in federal government jurisdictions and in most provinces. However, only the largest work places grant paid leave for parents to bond with newly adopted children. The most obvious reason is that adoption happens so seldom; in a small work place, the need for adoption leave rarely if ever arises.

Where adoption leave provisions exist, the benefits are usually similar to those for maternity and paternity leave. Adoptive parents have the same rights to unemployment insurance as birth mothers. (Only one parent is allowed to claim, however.)

The most common way of establishing adoption leave is to write a codicil into the maternity and paternity leave guidelines giving adoptive parents the same rights as birth parents. However, most employers do not establish a policy on adoption leave until they receive a request.

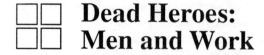 Dead Heroes: Men and Work

There is an abundant literature for women on how to combine work and family life, how to balance work and play and how to achieve personal wholeness. That literature does not yet have a counterpart directed towards men. Most of the literature for men pushes in the opposite direction: to be a winner as a male, a man is expected to give more and more to work—to become a super-workaholic.

On average, North American men die about eight years younger than their female counterparts. Most people wrongly assume that this gap is based on biological differences. In fact, prior to about 1800 the gap in life expectancy between men and women was quite small. In a good many cultures in the world, men live as long as women do.

Men in North America die young, not because of their biology but because of their behavior. The trends that have accompanied the women's movement offer further evidence of this fact. As more women join the ranks of the workaholics, they are starting to succumb to so-called male diseases: heart attacks, strokes and ulcers.

We men wear out before our time because of our one-sided pattern of behavior which is centred around compulsive overwork. However we try to rationalize it, the compulsion to work all the time is a slow form of suicide. In a way, we are like lemmings rushing headlong toward our own destruction.

What do you suppose these lemmings would say if we could interview them on their way to the sea? If the CBC were there with a microphone, the interview might go something like this.

"Excuse me! Could you tell our listeners why you're running into the sea?"

"Because you just can't buck the system."

"I'm the manager. I've got to set an example."

"I'm doing it for my wife and kids."

"Sorry, I don't have time to think about that, I've got a deadline to meet."

"Don't pick on me. I'm no different from anyone else."

"I have to keep up with my competition."

We can produce a whole raft of apparently rational, hard-nosed reasons why we have to work ourselves into early graves. But these so-called reasons are only excuses. The real reason for our behavior lies in our romantic vision of what it means to be a "man."

The Hero Myth

Underneath our apparent rationality, we are actually incurable romantics, and the romantic fantasy that most entrances us is the myth of the hero. These are the basic elements of the hero myth:

- Heroes can't die because they are protected by the forces of good.
- To succeed, heroes have to be tough and fearless.
- The hero who ignores his limits will have no limits.
- Heroes must struggle and suffer for a long time without recognition or reward.
- When he finally finds the Holy Grail, the hero will be loved and revered by all.

The hero myth is a wonderful, inspiring, uplifting fantasy. The problem is that we forget it's only a story based on wishful thinking. This is not so surprising given that we are constantly surrounded by wishful thinking, whether we are in the board room, the locker room, the lunch room or the TV room. John Wayne, Audie Murphy, James Bond, Rocky, Rambo — they are all the same story dressed up in different clothes.

The hero myth is a powerfully seductive fantasy. It tells us that no harm can come to us if we're on the side of goodness and right; that the man who acts as though he has no limits, has no limits; that life may be hell now, but once you rescue the fairy princess you'll receive half the kingdom. No wonder Sylvester Stallone can make the same movie over and over again and earn $100 million a pop. Hollywood knows how addicted we are to our fantasies.

There's a joke that says a lot about this issue. Two journalists are drinking in a bar at the top of a 40-story hotel. One says to the other, "You know, Mac, this is a very special building. It's designed so that if you fall off the edge the wind currents will pick you up and bring you back to the top." The second guy says " Aw, you're puttin' me on."

The first guy says, "I'll bet you a hundred dollars it's true." "You're on!" replies the other.

The first guy goes out on the balcony and jumps over the railing. He plummets toward the ground, then gradually slows to a halt, floats back up and lands gently on the balcony.

The second guy is awestruck. He hands over the $100 without a word. Then a glint appears in his eye, and he thinks, "I could make a fortune if I could do that trick."

He says to the first guy, "That's fantastic—let's both try it." They both climb up on the railing and jump off. The second guy plummets all the way down and goes SPLAT all over the pavement. The first falls halfway and then wafts back up to the balcony. He walks over to the bar, slaps down the $100 and orders another drink.

The bartender shakes his head and says, "You know, you can be a real jerk sometimes, Superman."

That joke is the story of our lives. We keep fooling ourselves into thinking we can do what Superman does, and then we go SPLAT all over the pavement. Take a look at the obituary column in your daily paper. There are a lot of us men pretending we're Superman and going SPLAT on the pavement at 60 or 50, and sometimes even at 40.

There is another analogy that illustrates the extent of male wishful thinking. Imagine that you own a little English sports car, a red MG, with a tachometer that redlines at about 6000 r.p.m. How would you treat that automobile?

You would probably drive with an engine speed in the 2000 to 4000 r.p.m. range because that would give you the smoothest ride and the best gas mileage and would create the least wear and tear on the engine. You might take it up to 5500 r.p.m. to pass or accelerate, but you wouldn't run it in that range for an extended period of time.

On rare occasions, you might take the engine right up to or even over the red line for a few minutes, just to see what the car can do. But you would be watching the tachometer closely and listening carefully to the engine. You would change the oil regularly and consider it a false economy to scrimp on preventive maintenance.

Now, consider how most of us treat our bodies, our biological sports cars. We continually drive our biological engines at 5500 r.p.m. because we foolishly believe that will make us stronger and more efficient. We regularly take ourselves well over the red line with our eyes closed because we think that if we don't see the red line, no red line exists. We skip preventive maintenance activities like sleep and vacations under the illusion that no harm will come to us because we are hard working and noble.

And we wonder why our MGs age more gracefully than we do!

The Virtue of Toughness

One part of the hero myth that deserves particular attention is the idea that heroes are supposed to be tough. Heroes are supposed to ignore fatigue and grit their teeth against pain. They are supposed to steel themselves against cowardice and rise above doubt and despair.

"Real men" are supposed to suppress negative emotions through sheer force of will. Actually, we rarely use willpower alone. That approach is probably workable for Superman, but mere mortals must rely on other techniques.

The most basic way that we suppress feelings is known as the startle response. "President John F. Kennedy has just been shot." Can you remember how your breath caught in your throat when you first heard that announcement? Central to the startle response is a sharp constriction of the chest muscles which numbs feeling and thereby dampens panic.

We have been conditioned to believe that we are not supposed to have certain feelings. Over the years, we tend to develop a chronic tightness in the chest—a kind of permanent startle response. Exercise is problematic because as soon as we start to breathe deeply, the chest opens up and we start to feel things we've been taught not to feel. As a result, we often find ourselves avoiding exercise without really knowing why.

Overeating is another way of suppressing "unmasculine" feelings. Whenever we eat something, our bodies release small amounts of endorphins—natural morphine-like substances which aid digestion by tranquilizing the emotions. Alcohol also works very effectively to depress the central nervous system. The nicotine in cigarettes and the caffeine in coffee both create a buzz in the nervous system which tends to obscure other feelings. We think of food, alcohol and cigarettes as addictive substances, but it's important to recognize that what we're really addicted to is the suppression of feeling. What is frightening about this wholesale suppression of feeling is how unconscious and automatic it is, and how deeply rooted. For a great many of us, feeling "normal" could more properly be described as feeling numb.

This learned pattern of suppressing feelings has some useful advantages in particular situations. Bursting into tears at a board meeting, for instance, is not likely to win us a promotion. It also enables us to deal with some awful but necessary tasks—like working in a slaughterhouse, for example. In emergency situations, it prevents us from succumbing to panic. And finally, it enables us temporarily to push ourselves beyond our normal limits.

The ability to suppress our feelings has some real advantages if used consciously in specific circumstances. But it has immense disadvantages if we do it automatically all the time. As a way of life, it has some fatal drawbacks, including:

loss of inner wisdom. Feeling and intuition add greatly to our power to make good decisions. Our emotions will often alert us to potential problems long before our reason sees anything wrong. When we habitually cut ourselves off from our feelings, we lose this emotional wisdom.

unsatisfactory relationships. People bond on a feeling level. Whether we're talking about a parent-child, husband-wife or friend-friend relationship, it will be lifeless if the channel to our feelings isn't open.

alienation from our bodies. Our bodies have intricate feedback mechanisms that tell us how to care for our bodies, what their needs are and what their limits are. Men make it a virtue to ignore all this crucial information. Then we wonder why we age so quickly.

damage to our bodies. The medical dangers of alcohol, nicotine and obesity are well known. Tense chest muscles constrict the heart and put it under extra strain. They also constrict breathing and leave the body chronically short of air. Cells that don't get enough oxygen are more at risk of becoming cancerous. Next time you see a John Wayne movie, watch how shallowly the Duke breathes. John Wayne died of cancer; the two things may not be unrelated.

loss of positive feelings. Unfortunately, the mechanisms that suppress feeling are non-selective. We lose good feelings as well as bad ones. When we try to be tough by suppressing negative or "unmasculine" feelings, we end up dead from the neck down. That's the real tragedy of men's lives. Too often our "heart" dies many years before we do.

As children, we experience life in full vibrant color, but little by little, our culture trains us to tune the color out. Often we end up living in black and white. We may even grow to believe that's all there is to life.

As a man, it's not easy to stay alive in our culture. Survival requires a conscious and continuous effort to break free of the male straight jacket. The following is a list of ways to take better care of yourself as a man.

Ten Ways to Save Your Own Life

1. If you live with lemmings, don't follow the crowd.

Our culture socializes men to kill themselves emotionally so they won't know they are killing themselves physically. A lot of our cultural role models, and much of the advice we get from the media, friends and co-workers, leads us to violate our real selves in pursuit of an unreal, idealized fantasy. An excellent guide to how to stop hurting yourself is *Compassion and Self-Hate* by Theodore Rubin.

2. Stop trying to be a hero.

The hero delusion is fool's gold—all glitter and no substance. It's a siren song that leads us to become dead heroes. In order to enjoy the pleasure of being ourselves, we must let go of our romantic fantasies. A thought-provoking book on the male myth is *He,* by Robert Johnson.

3. Get physical.

Body-centred activities are one way to revive feelings. Regular exercise, stretching, yoga, tai chi and outdoor recreation can all help focus attention on the body. If all else fails, breathe deeply.

4. Live more with less.

Our possessions possess us. How many of us own fancy cars or luxurious houses, only to find that we spend so much time working to pay for them that we're too tired to enjoy them? Doris Longacre's book, *Living More With Less* is an excellent guide to simplifying your life.

5. Seek balance.

Men tend to put all their eggs in one basket. A man who puts his whole life into his job is an excellent candidate for a heart attack when he retires or suicide if he loses his job. If you have several areas of meaning and satisfaction in your life—work, family, friends, hobbies and volunteering—your sense of self-esteem will stand on a much broader base.

6. Create safe spaces.

Many people will not support your efforts to become a feeling human being, so you need to seek out friends with whom you can be yourself. A men's support group can be a source of strength and comfort. Herb Goldberg's book *The New Male* is a useful item to keep on your bookshelf. A daily journal of thoughts and feelings is a private zone of safety.

7. Track your defences.

We block some of our feelings so quickly that the only way we can get in touch with them is by looking for the tracks they leave. Whenever you find yourself smoking, drinking or eating too much, begin to monitor your thoughts. What were you thinking just before you decided you needed a drink? This is one way to discover and face the feelings that you automatically avoid.

8. Nurture others — and yourself.

Women are generally better at taking care of themselves, partly because they get more practice in nurturing. When you practice giving attention to others and showing compassion for them, it's not so hard to extend the same attention and compassion to yourself. Gender roles are changing, however. It used to be the case that men produced and women nurtured. Now women are both producers and nurturers. This change takes part of the load off men as bread winners, but it also means that we must improve our nurturing skills in order to keep the gender seesaw in balance.

9. Value resilience over toughness.

When something is tough, it's strong but brittle. Push it past its limits and it shatters. On the other hand, something that is resilient immediately bounces back when pushed too far. In this sense, resilience means survival. To put it concretely, consider the difference between an egg and a tennis ball. If you try to depress the surface of an egg, it resists (it's tough), but it eventually breaks. The tennis ball gives way and comes back (it's resilient). Life tends to knock human beings around a certain amount. Which will fare better under pressure —

toughness, or resilience? If you admire Humpty Dumpty, model your-self after the egg. But if you would like to keep your bounce as the years go by, you'd better know how to give a little.

10. Work less.

The human body is not designed to work 50 to 80 hours per week on a regular basis. Most men can arrange to work less if they approach their employer in the right way. (This book shows you how!) Self-employed people who are overloaded should consider taking in a partner. Your business may be better off if you give it your best instead of your all.

The Flexible
Work Place

As more people demand reduced or flexible work schedules, organizations will have to adapt in order to attract and retain the most productive and highly qualified employees. A number of changes can facilitate the operation of the flexible work place:

CAFETERIA-STYLE BENEFITS

Many companies are finding that standardized benefit packages do not meet the diverse needs and wants of their employees. An alternate approach is to allow new employees to select their own benefit package from a range of possible choices. An employee's salary at any given time would comprise the gross hourly wage multiplied by the number of hours in a pay period, minus the cost of benefits. (Prior to the advent of the computer, this system would have been a nightmare to administer; now it's easy.)

With cafeteria-style benefits, employees can be fairly remunerated and have the benefit plan of their choice, regardless of the number of hours they work. Even temporary staff are treated fairly. (They usually keep their full gross hourly wage rather than signing up for benefits.) A cafeteria-style plan also more fairly remunerates employees who work overtime.

HOURS OF WORK COMMITTEE

When all work-scheduling issues go through one standing committee, it is easier to develop coherent policies. A single ongoing committee can develop more expertise and understanding of the issues than multiple ad hoc committees. A standing committee is also better able to monitor programs over time and to catch problems before they escalate. The committee should include representatives from labour, management and the personnel department. Often one member of the committee is empowered to act as an "umpire" to settle smaller disputes.

FLEXIBLE PENSION ARRANGEMENTS

Employees on reduced work schedules should be able to contribute to the pension plan as though they were working full-time. This is often essential if the employee is approaching retirement age. Pension plans which allow employees some flexibility in the amount they contribute and the size of their pension are an important part of any cafeteria-style benefit plan.

EFFICIENT USE OF MEETING TIME

A two-hour staff meeting takes up only five per cent of a full-time worker's week but 10 per cent of a half-time worker's week. The more people who work reduced hours the more important it is to conduct meetings efficiently. The predigesting of issues by small committees and the use of a timed agenda are useful mechanisms for keeping staff meetings short.

CROSS TRAINING OF STAFF

The more flexibility an organization offers its staff, the more often employees will be required to do one another's work. Cross training staff to cope with more than one job facilitates flexibility. It also promotes teamwork and better understanding between employees. It provides insurance if an employee gets sick suddenly or has an accident. In management positions, cross training prepares people to move up the ladder.

PERMANENT RELIEF STAFF

Leaves, V-Time and banked overtime programs all work best with a full-time permanent relief staff. A permanent relief staff means that backfill staff are competent, committed and well versed in the company culture.

SELF-DIRECTED STAFF

The more people work independently and organize their own hours the more important it becomes to train employees to manage themselves. John Naisbitt does an excellent job of discussing this issue in *Re-inventing the Corporation.*

FLAT PAY GRADIENTS

Pay differentials should be altered in a couple of ways. First, differences across occupations should be minimized if employees are going to stand in for one another more frequently. Second, casual and part-time employees should get the same total hourly remuneration (including benefits) as full-time workers. Otherwise, employers will try to expand the cheaper end of the gradient, and employees will gravitate to the expensive end of the gradient. We recommend prorated rather than full benefits for part-time staff.

ACCESSIBLE INFORMATION

More information should be stored in written form if employees are going to fill in for one another. Good message-taking habits need to be practised. Files must be returned to their original locations. Organizations with telecommuting staff find it helpful if most records are stored electronically.

EARNED TIME OFF

Once employees have the ability to bank time or make up for lost time, a paid sick leave program becomes unnecessary. Instead, the average amount of sick time per year is added to the employee's vacation allowance; this becomes "earned time off." Earned time off (ETO) can be used as sick leave or as vacation time. The ETO system rewards employees who stay healthy by allowing them extra vacation time; the usual system "rewards" employees who get sick by giving them paid time off. An ETO system gives all employees more equal treatment. Unscheduled absenteeism generally decreases on an ETO system, and planned vacations increase.

PROFESSIONAL DEVELOPMENT

If an employer wants a staff that stays and grows, ongoing training and career development should be offered to all employees. Vocational counselling, cross-training, in-service courses and paid educational leave can all be used to encourage professional development within an organization.

For a more complete discussion of the flexible work place, see John Naisbitt's *Re-inventing the Corporation*.

Further Resources

Step One: Thinking Clearly About Work

WORK IN THE PAST

Sahlins, Marshall. *Stone-Age Economics*. Hawthorne, NY: Aldine de Gruyter, 1972.

Terkel, Studs. *Working*. New York: Avon, 1983.

WORK IN THE FUTURE

Naisbitt, John and Aburdene, Patricia. *Re-inventing the Corporation: Transforming Your Job and Your Company for the New Information Society*. New York: Warner Books, 1985.

Yankelovich, Daniel. *New Rules: Searching for Self-Fulfillment in a World Turned Upside Down*. New York: Random, 1981.

Conference Board of Canada. *Attitudes Towards New Work Patterns*. 1986. Available from: The Conference Board of Canada, 255 Smythe Road, Ottawa, Ontario K1H 8M7.

Canadian Mental Health Association. *Work and Well-being: The Changing Realities of Employment*. 1984. Available from: The Canadian Mental Health Association, 2160 Yonge Street, Toronto, Ontario M4S 2Z3.

WOMEN AND WORK

Shaevitz, Marjorie. *The Superwoman Syndrome*. New York: Warner Books, 1985.

Lowman, Kaye. *Of Cradles and Careers: A Guide to Re-Shaping Your Job to Include a Baby in Your Life*. New York: NAL, Penguin, Inc., 1985.

Cassedy, Ellen and Nussbaum, Karen. *Nine to Five: The Working Woman's Guide to Office Survival*. Cleveland: Working Women Education Fund, 1983. Available from: National Assoc. for Working Women, 614 Cleveland Avenue N.W., Cleveland, OH 44113.

Shom-Moffat, Patti and Teffler, Cynthia. *The Women's Workbook.* Toronto: Between the Lines, 1983.

WORK AND FAMILY

Magid, Renee Y. *When Mothers and Fathers Work: Creative Strategies for Balancing Career and Family.* New York: AMACOM, American Management Association, 1987.

Canadian Employment and Immigration Advisory Council. *Workers With Family Responsibilities in a Changing Society: Who Cares.* A report presented to the Minister of Employment and Immigration. Ottawa: Supplies and Services Canada, 1987.

Johnson, Laura C., Klein, Elka and Paperny, Cathy. *The Working Families Project: Sourcebook on Work-Related Day Care in Canada.* 1985. Available from: The Social Planning Council of Metro Toronto, 950 Yonge Street, Toronto, Ontario M5E 1V8.

Step Two: Surveying Your Options (see Step Five)

Step Three: Choosing Your Time

CAREER CHANGES/LIFE DIRECTIONS

Bolles, Richard. *What Color is Your Parachute?* Berkeley: Ten Speed Press, 1986.

Bolles, Richard. *The Three Boxes of Life: How to Get Out of Them.* Berkeley: Ten Speed Press, 1981.

Sher, Barbara and Gottlieb, Annie. *Wishcraft: How to Get What You Really Want.* New York: Ballantine, 1983.

ASSERTIVENESS

Smith, Manuel J. *When I Say No, I Feel Guilty.* New York: Bantam, 1985.

Paul, Jordan and Margaret. *Do I Have to Give Up Me to be Loved by You?* Minneapolis: CompCare Pubns., 1983.

STRESS MANAGEMENT

Hanson, Peter. *The Joy of Stress.* 1986. Available from: Hanson Stress Management Organization, 5 Thornburg Crescent, Islington, Ontario M9A 2M1.

TIME MANAGEMENT

Lakein, Alan. *How to Get Control of Your Time and Your Life.* New York: NAL, Penguin, Inc., 1974.

PERFECTIONISM

Rubin, Theodore. *Compassion and Self-Hate.* New York: Macmillan, 1986 (revised edition).

Step Four: Deciding About Money

MONEY

Longacre, Doris. *Living More With Less.* Scottsdale, PA: Herald Press, 1980.

BENEFITS

Campling, Robert F. *Employee Benefits and the Part-Time Worker.* School of Industrial Relations Research Essay Series No.13. Kingston: Industrial Relations Centre, Queen's University, 1987.

Catalyst. *Flexible Benefits: How to Set Up a Plan When Your Employees are Complaining, Your Costs are Rising and You're Too Busy to Think About It.* New York: Catalyst, 1986.

Step Five: Designing a Program

JOB SHARING

Olmsted, Barney and Smith, Suzanne. *The Job Sharing Handbook.* New York: Penguin, 1983.

Meier, Gretl S. *Job-Sharing: A New Pattern for Quality of Work and Life.* Kalamazoo, MI: W.E.Upjohn Institute for Employment Research, 1979.

Moorman, Barbara, Smith, Suzanne, and Ruggels, Suzie. *Job Sharing in the Schools.* San Francisco: New Ways To Work, 1980.

Moorman, Barbara. *Job Sharing Through Collective Bargaining.* San Francisco: New Ways To Work, 1982.

McGuire, Nan and Olmsted, Barney. *Job Sharing in Health Care.* San Francisco: New Ways To Work, 1984.

State of Wisconsin. *Project JOIN Final Report, A Demonstration Project to Develop and Test a Job Sharing and Flexible Time Arrangement in the Wisconsin Civil Service.* State of Wisconsin, Department of Employment Relations, 1979.

PERMANENT PART-TIME

Rothberg, Diane S. and Ensor Cook, Barbara. *Part-time Professional.* Washington: Acropolis Books Ltd., 1985.
Wallace, Joan (Commissioner). *Part-time Work In Canada. Report of the Commission of Inquiry into Part-time Work.* Ottawa: Labour Canada, 1983.
Nollen, Stanley D. and Martin, Virginia, H. *Alternative Work Schedules: Part 2: Permanent Part-time Employment.* New York: AMACOM, American Management Association, 1978.

LEAVES OF ABSENCE

Abrams, Don. *The Time Buyer: How To Get Time Off Your Job Without Loss of Income.* Toronto: Deneau, 1986.
Van Moltke, Konrad and Schneevoight, Norbert. *Educational Leaves: European Experience for American Consideration.* San Francisco: Jossey-Bass, 1977.
Catalyst. *The Corporate Guide to Parental Leaves.* New York: Catalyst, 1987.

V-TIME

Moorman, Barbara and Olmsted, Barney. *V-Time: A New Way to Work.* San Francisco: New Ways To Work, 1985.

BANKED OVERTIME

Donner, Arthur (Chairman). *Working Times: The Report of the Ontario Task Force on Hours of Work and Overtime.* Toronto: Ontario Ministry of Labour, 1987.

PHASED RETIREMENT

Swank, Constance. *Phased Retirement: The European Experience.* Washington: National Council for Alternative Work Patterns, 1982.

Rostow, Jerome and Zager, Robert. *The Future of Older Workers in America: New Options for an Extended Working Life*. Scarsdale, NY: Work in America Institute, 1980.

Paul, Carolyn E. *Expanding Part-time Work Options for Older Americans: A Feasibility Study*. Los Angeles: Employment and Retirement Division, Ethel Percy Andrus Gerontology Center, University of Southern California, 1983.

Dennis, Helen. *Retirement Preparation: What Retirement Specialists Need to Know*. Lexington, MA: Lexington Books, D.C. Heath and Company, 1984.

Page, Cynthia L. *Your Retirement: How to Plan for a Secure Future*. New York: Action for Older Persons, Inc., Acro Publishing Inc., 1984.

Jacobson, Beverly. *Young Programs for Older Workers: Case Studies in Progressive Personnel Policies*. New York: Van Nostrand Reinhold/Work in America Institute Series, 1980.

FLEXITIME

Silverstein, Pam and Srb, Jozetta H. *Flexitime: Where, When, and How*. Ithaca, NY: ILR Press, 1987.

Simcha, Ronen. *Flexible Working Hours: An Innovation in the Quality of Working Life*. New York: McGraw-Hill, 1980.

Stanley D. Nollen and Martin, Virginia. *Alternative Work Schedules, Part 1: Flexitime*. New York: AMACOM, 1978.

COMPRESSED WORK WEEK

Poor, Riva. *4 Days, 40 Hours: Reporting a Revolution in Work and Leisure*. Cambridge, MA: Burske and Poor, 1970.

Stanley Nollen and Martin, Virginia H. *Alternative Work Schedules, Part 3: Compressed Work Week*. New York: AMACOM, 1978.

TELECOMMUTING

Gordon, Gil and Kelly, Marcia. *Telecommuting: How to Make It Work for You and Your Company*. Englewood Cliffs, NY: Prentice-Hall, 1986.

Atkinson, William. *Working at Home: Is it For You?* Homewood, IL: Dow Jones-Irwin, 1985.

Arden, Lynie. *The Worksteader News*, 2396 Coolidge Way, Rancho Cordova, CA, 95670.

Telespan Publishing. *Telecommuting Review: the Gordon Report.*
Available from: Telespan Publishing, 50A West Palm St.,
Altadena, CA, 91001.

HOME WORK

Ellison, Tom and Susan. *The Whole Work Catalogue: Options for More
Rewarding Work.* 1986. Available from: The New Careers
Center, 6003 North 51st Street, Box 297 CT, Boulder, CO
80306.
Arden, Lynie. *The Work-at-Home Sourcebook.* 1987. Available from:
Live Oak Publishing, 6003 North 51st Street, Number 105,
P.O. Box 2193, Boulder, CO, 80306.
Gillis-Zetterberg, Carol. *Working at Home.* 1985. Available from the
author: 129 West Marshall Avenue, Langhorne, PA 19047.

Step Six: Getting What You Want

CASE STUDIES

McCarthy, Maureen and Rosenberg, Gail S. *Work Sharing: Case
Studies.* Kalamazoo, MI: W.E. Upjohn Institute for
Employment Research, 1981.
Johnson, Laura C. *Working Families: Workplace Supports for Families.*
Toronto: Social Planning Council of Metropolitan Toronto,
1986.
Nollen, Stanley D. *New Work Schedules in Practice: Managing Time in
a Changing Society.* New York: Van Nostrand/Reinhold, 1982.

LEGAL CONSIDERATIONS

CCH Canadian Limited. *Canadian Master Labour Guide: A Guide to
Canadian Labour Law.* Don Mills, Ontario: CCH Canadian
Limited, 1987.

EMPLOYER ATTITUDES

Peters, Thomas J. *In Search of Excellence: Lessons from America's
Best-Run Companies.* New York: Harper & Row, 1982.
Rogers, Judy. *Attitudes Towards Alternative Work Arrangements: A
Qualitative Assessment Among Employers in Metropolitan
Toronto.* Toronto: Social Planning Council of Metropolitan
Toronto, 1986.

Step Seven: Putting Work In Its Place

NEGOTIATING

Fisher, Roger and Ury, William. *Getting to Yes: Negotiating Agreement Without Giving In*. Boston: Houghton Mifflin, 1981.

ORGANIZATIONS

Society for Work Options, c/o FOCUS, 509 10th Avenue East, Seattle, Washington 98102.

Association for Part-time Professionals, P.O. Box 3419, Alexandria, Virginia 22302.

New Ways to Work, 149 Ninth Street, San Francisco, California, 94103. (415) 552-1000.

Work Options Niagara, 173 Niagara Street, St. Catharines, Ontario L2R 4M1 (416) 684-1195.

Catalyst: National Network of Career Resource Centres, 250 Park Avenue South, New York, NY 10003.

Work Well, Suite 521, 620 View Street, Victoria, B.C. V8W 1J6. (604) 385-2201

The Leisure and Life Quality Institute, The Lumbers Bldg., Faculty of Environmental Studies, York University, 4700 Keele Street, North York, Ontario M3J 1P3.

Canadian Association of Pre-Retirement Planners, c/o Rein Selles, Alberta Council on Aging, 390 - 10665 Jasper Avenue, Edmonton, Alberta, T5J 3S9.

Canadian Association of Retired Persons, c/o 27 Queen Street East, Suite 304, Toronto, Ontario M5C 2M6.

Ethel Percy Andrus Gerontology Center, Employment and Retirement Division, Ethel Percy Andrus Gerontology Center, University of Southern California, University Park, MC0191, Los Angeles, CA 90089-0191.

WORK WELL PUBLICATIONS
Suite 521 - 620 View Street
Victoria, B.C., Canada V8W 1J6
(604) 385-2201

OPTIONS AT WORK, Case Study Series: Profiles of Flexible Work Schedules in Practice. Victoria: Work Well, 1988. Six issues/year: $20.00 Cdn. Single issue: $4.00

The profiles in this series include:
- public and private sector examples.
- programs involving large and small employers.
- comprehensive programs and individual plans.
- work schedules that address issues of turnover, peak coverage, layoffs and special health needs.

WORC Well: A Guide to Creating Worktime Options Resource Centres, by Bruce O'Hara. Toronto: Canadian Mental Health Association, 1987. 76 pages. $15.00 Cdn.

- An overview of available work options.
- Detailed descriptions of Work Option Resource Centre services.
- A step-by-step guide to establishing a Work Option Resource Centre.

PUT WORK IN ITS PLACE: How to Redesign Your Job to Fit Your Life, by Bruce O'Hara. Victoria: Work Well, 1988. 260 pages. $12.95 Cdn.

This complete guide to the flexible work place includes:
- information on job sharing, permanent part-time, leaves, V-Time, banked overtime, phased retirement, flexitime, compressed work week and telecommuting.
- exercises to sort out your needs for time and money.
- help in designing and proposing a new work schedule.

Bulk order rates available on request.

A second edition of *Put Work In Its Place* is planned. We would appreciate your help in improving our book.

The most helpful sections were: _____

_____

_____

_____

_____

In the next edition I would suggest the following changes:

_____

_____

_____

_____

Please return to:

Work Well
Suite 521 - 620 View Street
Victoria, B.C.
V8W 1J6

If you were successful in negotiating a new work schedule, please fill out the next page.

Work Well acts as a resource for those interested in Canadian examples of flexible work schedules.

Are you using an alternative work schedule?

Description of option: _____

_____

_____

Job Title_____

_____

Name _____

Address _____

_____

_____ postal code _____

Phone: _____(work) _____(home)

Please return to:

Work Well
Suite 521 - 620 View Street
Victoria, B.C.
V8W 1J6